THE METRIC SYSTEM OF MEASUREMENT

Verda Holmberg

Copyright © 1975

Activity Resources Company, Inc.
P.O. Box 4875
Hayward, California 94540
(415) 278-8178

Typeset by Vera Allen Composition Service, Hayward, California

PREFACE

This workbook contains pages of enrichment about the metric system of measurement. Experiences are offered with —

> linear measurement,
> area and volume measurement,
> liquid capacity and mass measurement,
> and temperature measurement.

all in the language of the metric system. Another section near the end of the book relates the Metric System to the U.S. Customary System. Included in section 2 are materials to further the understanding of a number system based on ten, place value, notation with exponents, and operations with the powers of the base. These materials help the student relate our Decimal Number System to the Metric Measurement System.

The pages are arranged in mini units of study so that one unit may be used over several days. It is also possible to select just certain pages and use them in connection with the basic text in the regular program throughout the school year.

The materials were written for an ability range of easy to difficult for upper elementary students. Much of the material could be used in intermediate levels for students who have had little or no work on the metric system.

Much material is now being printed concerning Systems International — SI, the metric system. It is difficult for teachers to study it all. The following materials are helpful to the teacher and to the student. They are rather inexpensive and easily obtained. Best of all they are readable and contain excellent suggestions and information.

Thanks to Betty Leister and Janis Holmberg for illustrations.

VH

SUGGESTED READING

A METRIC AMERICA: A DECISION WHOSE TIME HAS COME U.S.
    S. D. Catalogue #13.10-345 $2.25. U.S. Government Printing Office,
    Washington, D.C.: GPO, 1972

A METRIC HANDBOOK FOR TEACHERS, Jon L. Higgins, (Editor), 1974.
    National Council of Teachers of Mathematics,
    1906 Association Drive, Reston, VA 22091

TABLE OF CONTENTS

SECTION ONE — Metric Linear Measurement   1-22
- Take Your Choice . . . 2-3
- Relationship mm, cm, dm, m . . . 4-8
- Activities Measuring Lines . . . 9-11
- The Measuring Wheel . . . 12-13
- Pt. to Pt. . . . 14
- Scale and the Dictionary . . . 15
- Scale and the km . . . 16-17
- Perimeter in Metric . . . 18
- Slide Metric for + and − . . . 19-20
- Extra Activities in Metric Line Measurement . . . 21

SECTION TWO — Place Value and Metric   23-36
- Based on Ten Chart . . . 24-25
- Abacus with Place Value . . . 26-27
- A Just-Suppose Money System . . . 28
- Relation to the Whole — Decimal Form . . . 29-31
- X & ÷ by 10, 100, 1000 . . . 32-33
- Exponents . . . 34-36

SECTION THREE — Metric Area Measurement   37-52
- cm^2 and dm^2 — The Area . . . 38
- Plot the Square Numbers . . . 39
- mm^2 . . . 40
- Areas and Perimeters . . . 41
- Metric Geoboard . . . 42-43
- On the cm Grid . . . 44-45
- Metric Tangrams . . . 46
- Area, Perimeters, Length, Width . . . 47
- Areas — Small and Large . . . 48-49
- Nomograph for Areas . . . 50-51
- Extra Activities in Metric Area Measurement . . . 52

SECTION FOUR — Metric Volume Measurement   53-58
- Space Measurement — cm^3, dm^3 . . . 54-55
- Building Packages . . . 56
- Build a Cube — Powers of the Base . . . 57
- Extra Activities in Metric Volume Measurement . . . 58

SECTION FIVE — Metric Liquid Capacity Measurement 59-64
   The Liter 60-61
   To Measure a Liter, l 62-63
   What is Capacity 64

SECTION SIX — Metric Mass Measurement 65-70
   Mass: The Gram, g 66
   Compare the Gram to Other Units 67
   Make & Use a Balance 68-69
   Extra Activities in Liquid & Mass Measurement 70

SECTION SEVEN — Metric: U.S. Customary Compared 71-82
   Temperature — Celsius 72-73
   Converter — Length cm ↔ in 74
   Converter — Mass & Length km ↔ lb, cm ↔ in 75
   Converter — Mass & Liquid g ↔ oz, l ↔ oz 76-77
   Converter — Length km ↔ mi 78
   Computing — Metric & U.S. Customary 79
   Tables of Metric ↔ U.S. Customary 80-81
   Which Measurement to Use 82

SECTION EIGHT — Enrichment in Metric 83-90
   The Metroscope for + & − 84-85
   Metric Word Puzzles 86-87
   Crossnumber Puzzle 88
   Area Puzzle 89

SECTION NINE — The Answers 91-98

Metric Length Measurement

SECTION ONE

TAKE YOUR CHOICE –

Pick any small segment you wish:
    Width of your finger
    Length of your printed name
    Width of a bean
    A piece of a drinking straw
    A piece of a toothpick
Use your segment as a unit to find the measure of the path from ZIG to ZOG through ZAG.

Try a different sized segment.

Is it the same distance?

Compare your number with others' measures.

Measure other lines around your classroom with your unit.

Would your measure agree with everyone else?

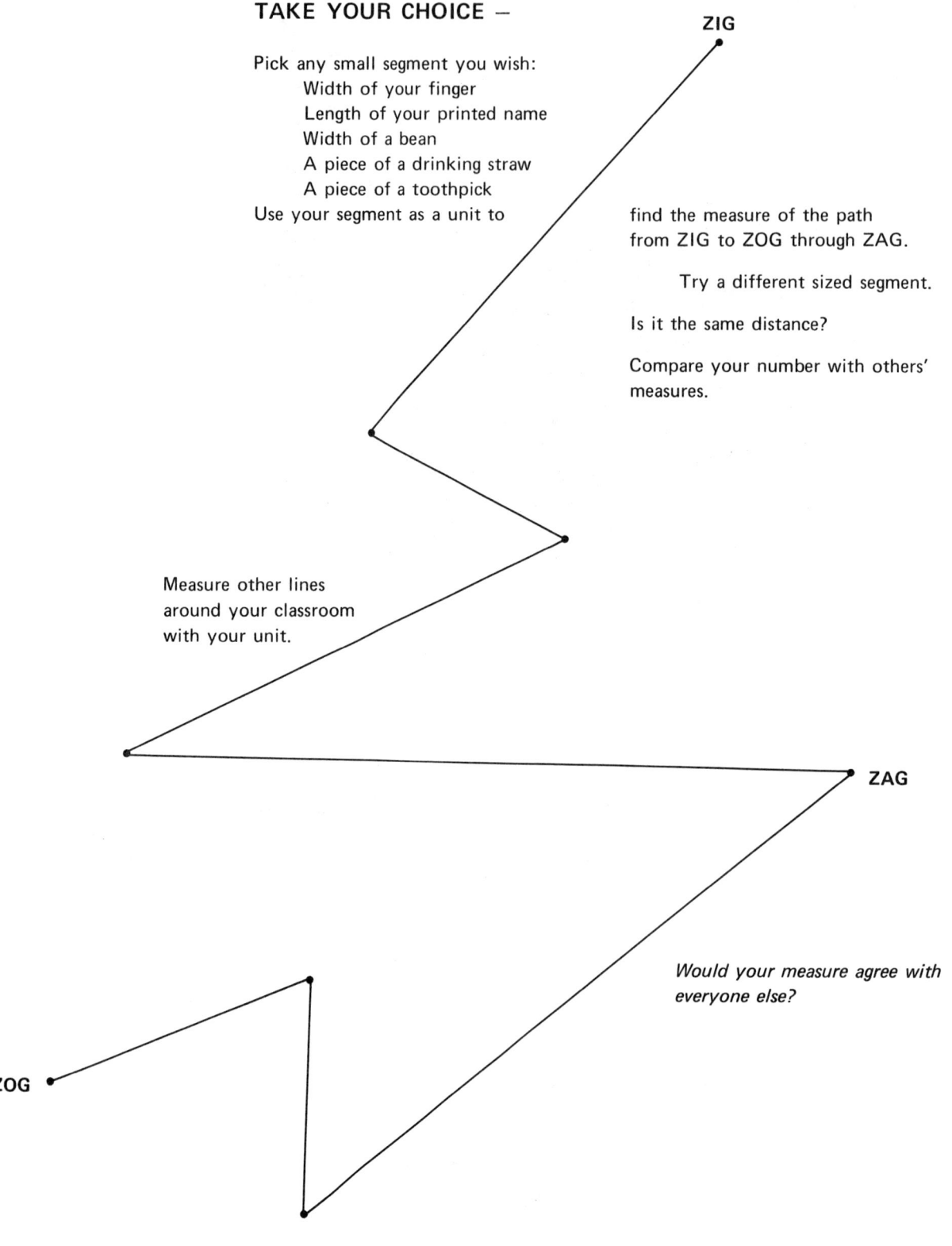

TAKE YOUR CHOICE

Pick a small piece of flatness — a simple closed curve* — to use as a a unit for measuring this region.

What is your measure?

Does it agree with others?

Do we need a unit of measure that would be the same for everybody?

*Outline a bean
Copy a pattern from a shirt or dress cloth design.
Draw an amoeba — like a blob
Something else?

MEASUREMENTS IN AGREEMENT (Standard Measure)

The Centimeter cm of the metric system Used Round the World, SI*

Use a cm ruler to find the measurements to the nearest cm.

Segment	Measurement
$\overline{AB}$	_____
$\overline{DE}$	_____
$\overline{FG}$	_____
$\overrightarrow{HI}$	_____
$\overline{JK}$	_____
$\overline{LM}$	_____
$\overline{NO}$	_____
$\overline{PQ}$	_____

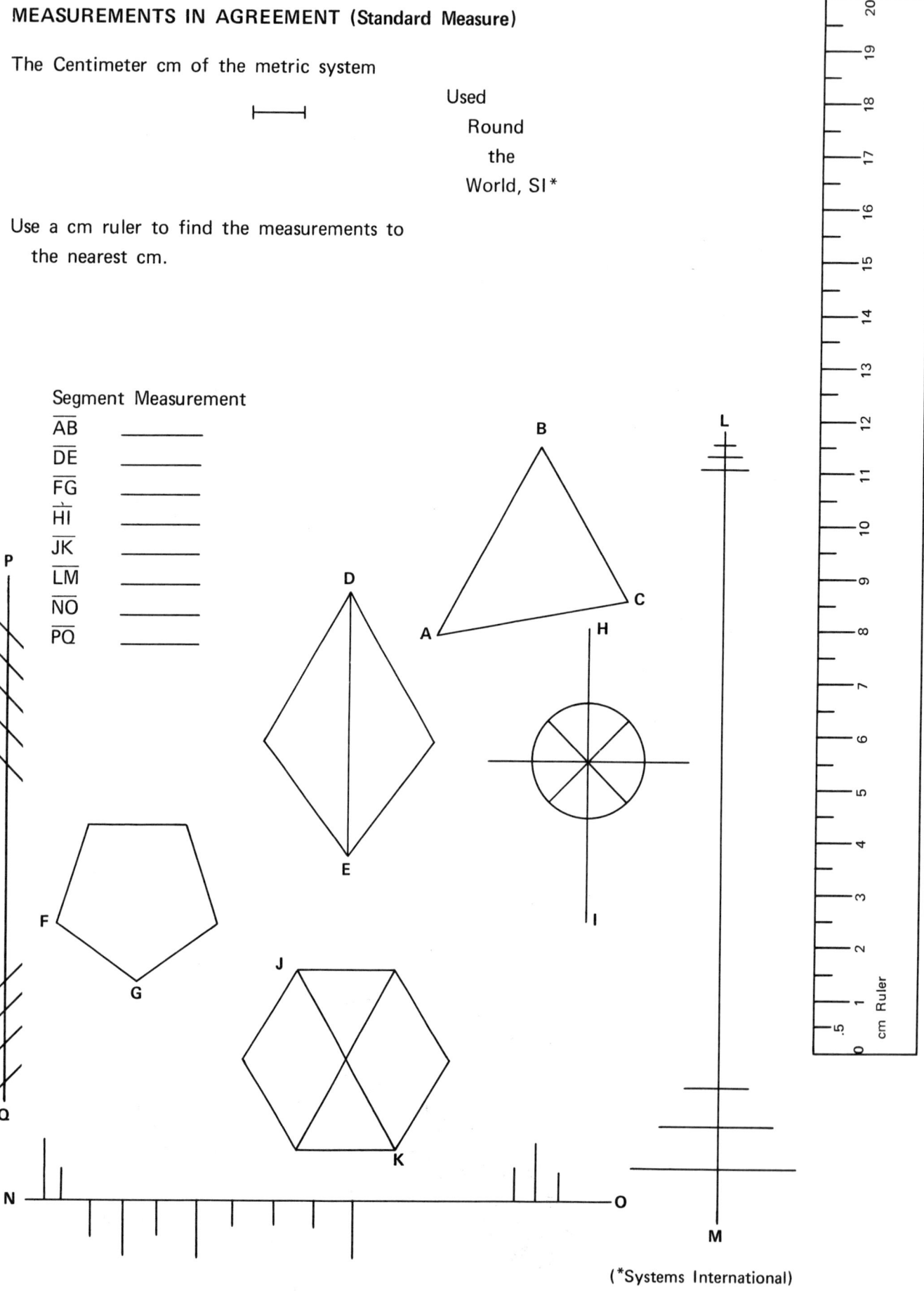

(*Systems International)

THE MILLIMETER mm

Use a mm ruler to measure these segments in mm.

$\overline{AB}$ _____
$\overline{BC}$ _____
$\overline{CD}$ _____
$\overline{DE}$ _____
$\overline{EF}$ _____
$\overline{FG}$ _____
$\overline{GH}$ _____
$\overline{HI}$ _____
$\overline{IJ}$ _____

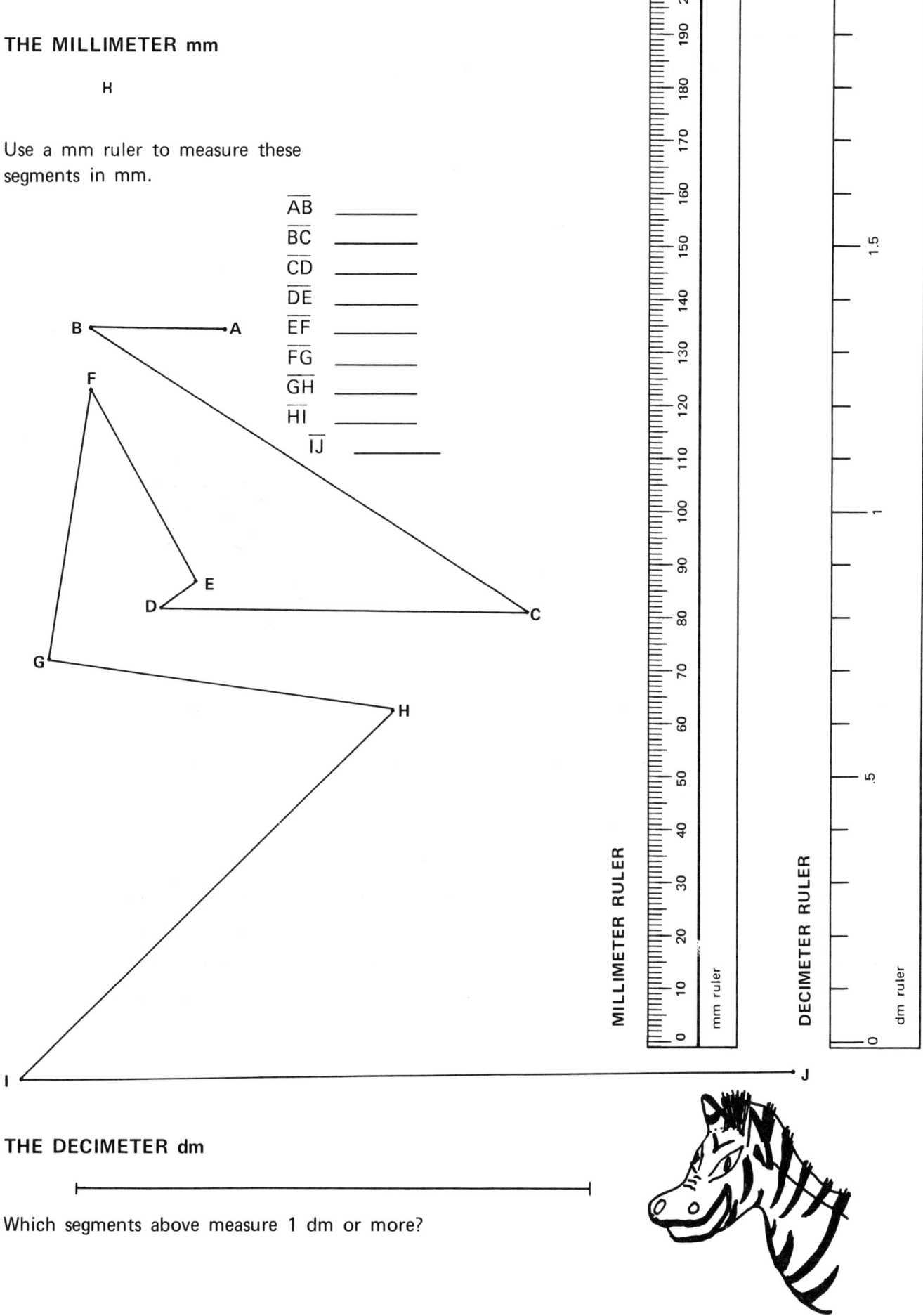

THE DECIMETER dm

Which segments above measure 1 dm or more?

RELATIONSHIP mm, cm, dm

Use the dm, cm, mm rulers to find relationships among dm, cm, and mm.

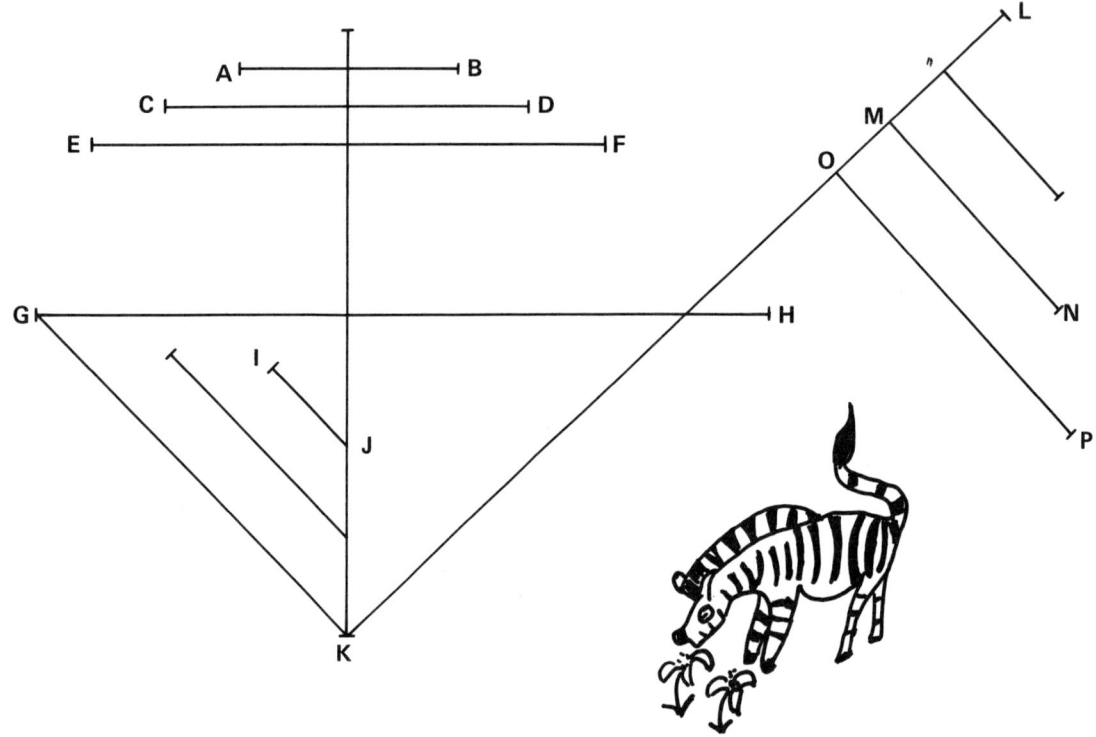

SEGMENT	mm	cm	dm
$\overline{AB}$			.3
$\overline{CD}$			
$\overline{EF}$			
$\overline{GH}$			
$\overline{IJ}$			.15
$\overline{KL}$		12.1	
$\overline{MN}$			
$\overline{OP}$	47		

RELATIONSHIP mm, cm, dm

Use the 3 rulers — mm, cm, dm —

Fill in the following:

a) 1 dm = _____ cm   1 cm = _____ mm

    2 dm = _____ cm   10 cm = _____ mm

    1 dm = _____ mm   4 cm = _____ mm

    2 dm = _____ mm   _____ cm = __150__ mm

    _____ cm = __180__ mm   8 cm = _____ mm

b) _____ cm = __180__ mm   1.1 cm = _____ mm

    _____ dm = __140__ mm   _____ cm = __95__ mm

    4.7 cm = _____ mm   6.2 cm = _____ mm

c) 5 dm = _____ cm   70 cm = _____ dm

    _____ dm = __110__ cm   93 cm = _____ mm

    _____ dm = __700__ mm   _____ cm = __630__ mm

    1.5 dm = _____ cm   _____ dm = __38__ cm

    3.7 dm = _____ mm   450 mm = _____ dm

Complete a line design using your ruler. Measure some of your segments.

THE METER

This is a meter, m. Connect all together!!

———————————————————————————————— 1 dm = 10 cm = 100 mm
—————————————————————————————— 2
———————————————————————————— 3
—————————————————————————— 4
———————————————————————— 5
—————————————————————— 6
———————————————————— 7
—————————————————— 8
———————————————— 9
—————————————— 10 dm = 1 m

Scale: |—| 1 dm

THE METER

1	m =	10	dm =	100	cm =	1000	mm
6	m =	_____	dm =	_____	cm =	_____	mm
15	m =	_____	dm =	_____	cm =	_____	mm
38	m =	_____	dm =	_____	cm =	_____	mm
.5	m =	_____	dm =	_____	cm =	_____	mm
2.7	m =	_____	dm =	_____	cm =	_____	mm
_____	m =	_____	dm =	480	cm =	_____	mm
_____	m =	9	dm =	_____	cm =	_____	mm
_____	m =	_____	dm =	_____	cm =	5750	mm
.060	m =	_____	dm =	_____	cm =	_____	mm

Activities with m, dm, cm, mm

Use your rulers, meter stick, or meter tape measure to find the measurements of things around you. (A length of string can be used instead of a tape measure.)

The width of this page _____

The length of this page _____

The length of your pencil _____

The length of the teacher's desk _____

The width of the door _____

Your height _____

Your waist _____

Your foot length _____

Your foot width _____

Around your head _____

Your hand spread _____

Your thumb length _____

Your wrist _____

Your ankle _____

Longest hair in class _____

Shortest piece of chalk _____

Length of gum wrapper _____

Distance around a bottle or jar _____

Gather some measurements about any one of the above from other students and graph the results.

RULER DESIGN

Use your dm, cm & mm rulers and the compass rose to finish the following design. You will reach a point with each segment.

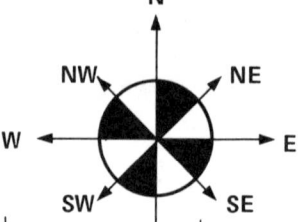

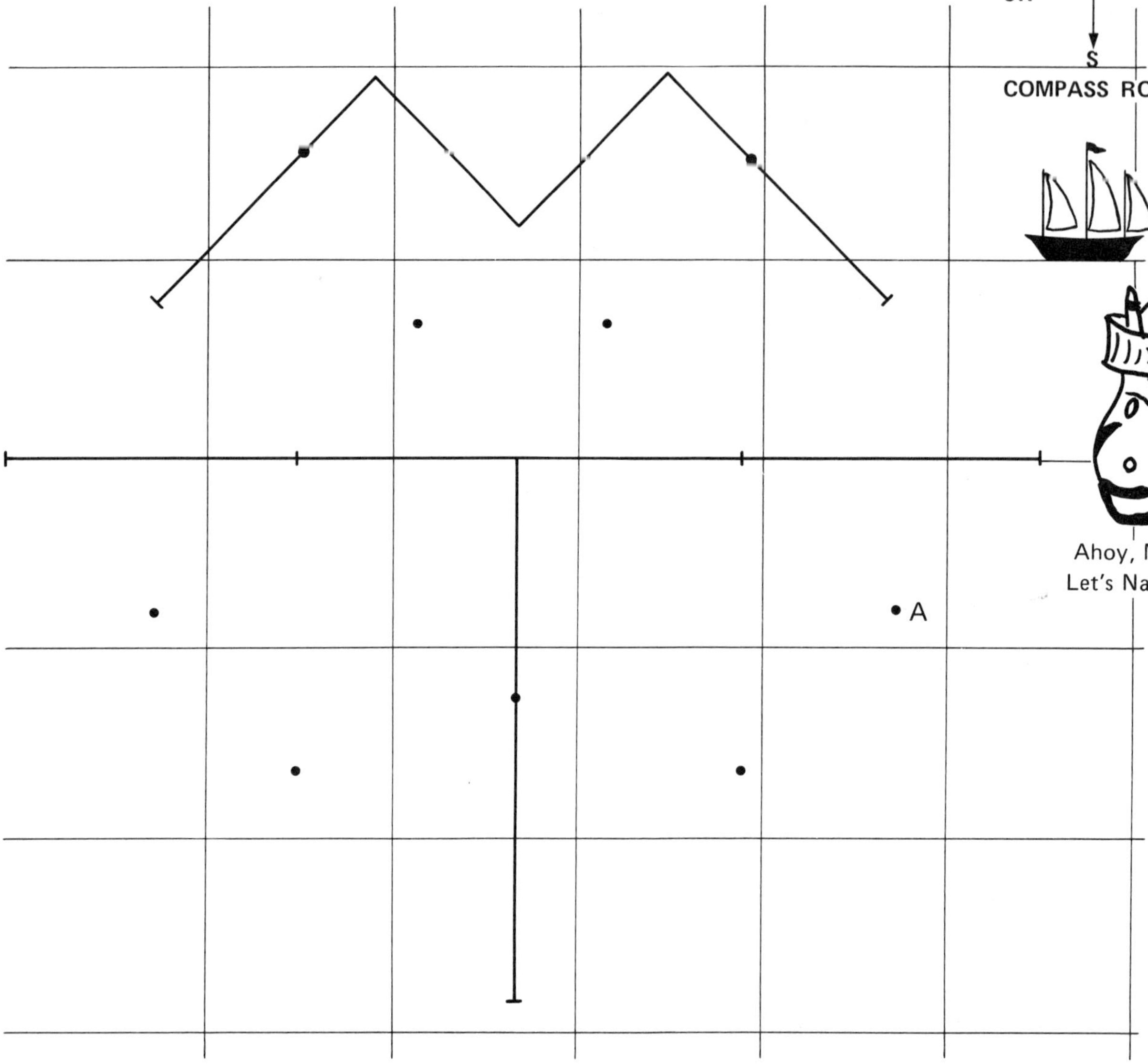

COMPASS ROSE

Ahoy, Mate
Let's Navigate

Use metric rulers and compass rose. Begin at point A. Connect these segments.

1. ↙	75 mm	6. ↙	30 mm	11. ↗	34 mm	16. ↘	30 mm
2. ↓	32 mm	7. ↗	75 mm	12. ↖	45 mm	17. ↑	42 mm
3. ↗	5.3 cm	8. ↘	3.4 cm	13. ↓	4.3 cm	18. ↘	5.3 cm
4. ↓	.85 dm	9. ↗	.45 dm	14. ↗	6.0 cm	19. ↑	3.2 cm
5. ↗	6 cm	10. ↙	4.5 cm	15. ↗	.3 dm	20. ↙	75 mm

16

Metric System of Measurement © Activity Resources Co. Hayward, CA 94540

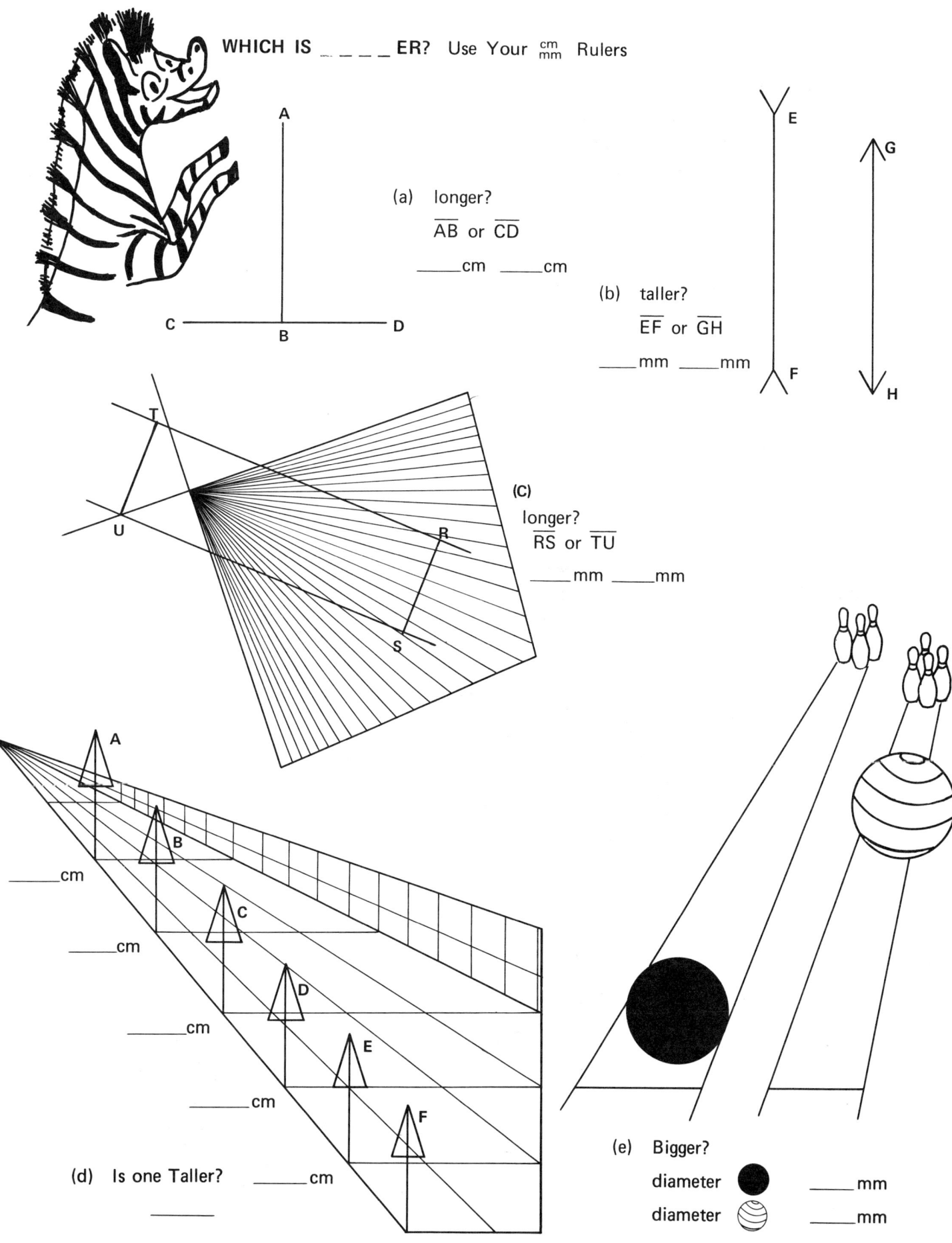

Use a measuring wheel —

Cut out the 1 dm (10 cm) wheel. Paste on a cardboard circle of same size. Use a pin to put a hole through the center. Remove pin and push through the end of a paper clip that has been bent out.

Roll the wheel along the pathways and measure to the nearest cm.

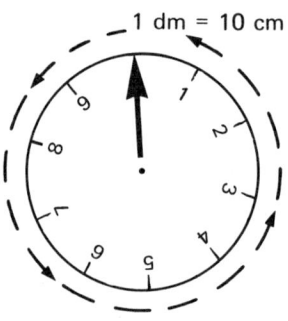

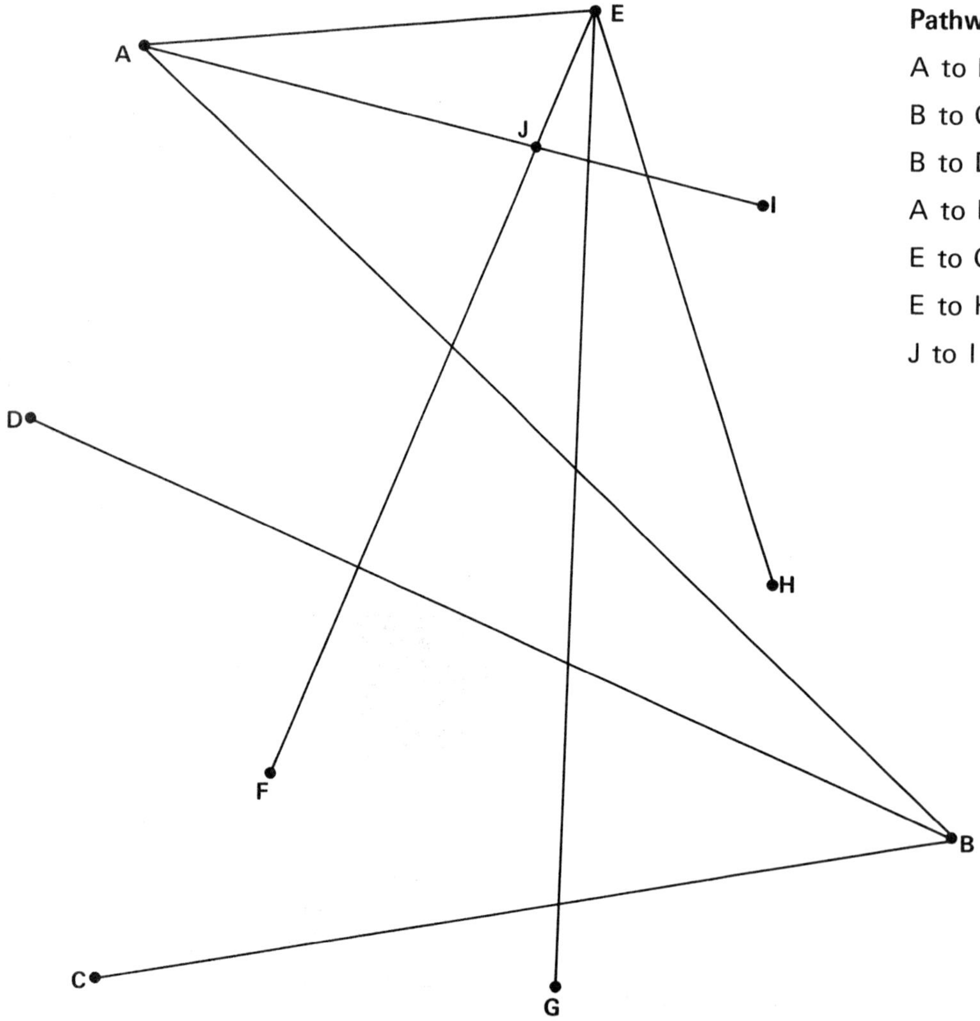

Pathway Measurement

A to B _____ dm

B to C _____ dm

B to D _____ dm

A to E to F _____ cm

E to G _____ mm

E to H _____ mm

J to I _____ dm

18

Metric System of Measurement © Activity Resources Co. Hayward, CA 94540

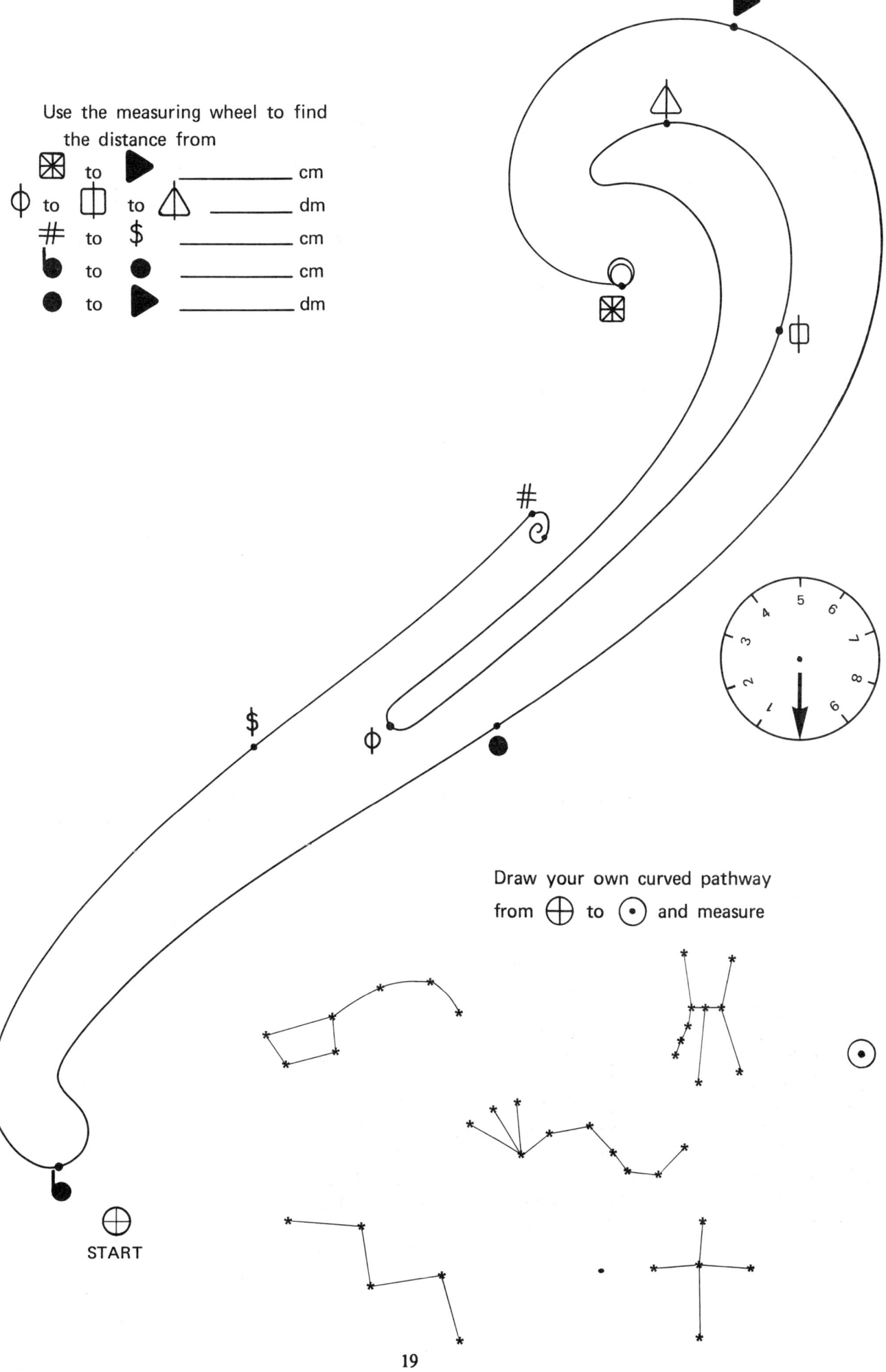

POINT TO POINT

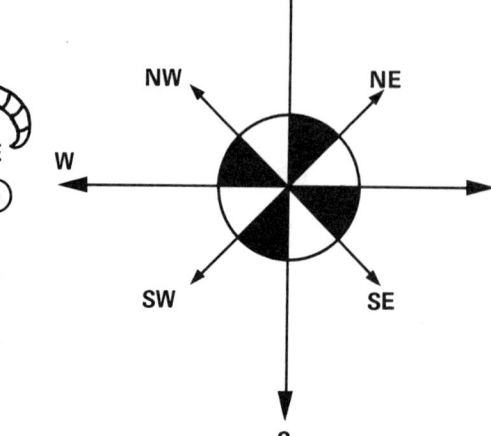

Cardinal points on the Compass Rose are
North
South
East
West

A cm worm can crawl along only those segments that follow the four cardinal directions on the Compass Rose. (No diagonals) Follow the trails of each worm as they leave their starting positions to meet at ✵

	SW	
(1)	E	4cm
(2)	N	10mm
(3)	W	3cm
(4)	N	1cm
(5)	E	20mm
(6)	N	10mm
(7)	W	3cm
(8)	N	1cm
(9)	E	30mm
(10)	N	2cm
(11)	E	2cm
(12)	S	10mm

TOTAL _____ cm
_____ mm

	NE	
(1)	W	20mm
(2)	S	3cm
(3)	E	1cm
(4)	S	20mm
(5)	W	10mm
(6)	S	2cm
(7)	W	1cm
(8)	N	20mm
(9)	W	1cm
(10)	S	2cm
(11)	W	10mm
(12)	N	2cm

_____ cm
_____ mm

	NW	
(1)	E	10mm
(2)	S	1cm
(3)	W	1cm
(4)	S	1cm
(5)	E	20mm
(6)	N	10mm
(7)	E	2cm
(8)	S	2cm
(9)	E	10mm
(10)	N	3cm
(11)	E	10mm
(12)	S	50mm
(13)	W	1cm

_____ cm
_____ mm

	SE	
(1)	W	2cm
(2)	N	2cm
(3)	W	1cm
(4)	S	20mm
(5)	W	10mm
(6)	N	20mm
(7)	W	2cm
(8)	N	3cm
(9)	E	1cm

_____ cm
_____ mm

SCALE

The dictionary uses pictures to help with their definitions. A fraction is usually given near the picture to indicate the size of the picture compared to the real thing. Measure the picture in mm or cm and figure the size of the real thing. Choose your answer from the bottom of the page by taking the measure closest to your number.

Puffin $\left(\frac{1}{10}\right)$

(a) A puffin is _____ cm.

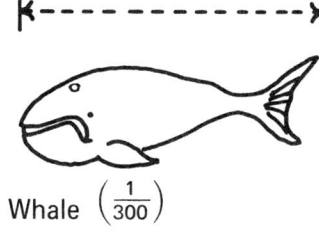

Whale $\left(\frac{1}{300}\right)$

(d) A whale is _____ m.

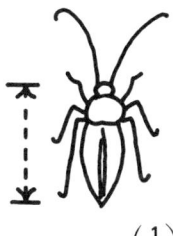

Cockroach $\left(\frac{1}{2}\right)$

(b) A cockroach is _____ cm.

Sea Horse $\left(\frac{1}{4}\right)$

(c) A sea horse is _____ mm.

(e) An antelope is _____ m.

Antelope $\left(\frac{1}{50}\right)$

Albatross $\left(\frac{1}{35}\right)$

(g) An albatross is _____ cm.

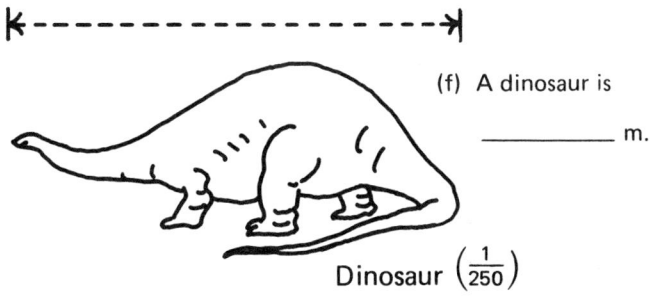

(f) A dinosaur is _____ m.

Dinosaur $\left(\frac{1}{250}\right)$

98,   30,   100,   12,   3.0,   15,   1.25

LARGER THAN M

Scale
1 dm = 10 cm

10 m = 1 dekameter dam
100 m = 1 hectometer hm
1000 m = 1 kilometer km

THE METER

Make a meter stick. Cut out 10 dm strips

1 dm

PASTE

from tag or cardboard. Paste together.

Use the meter to measure long or tall objects in the room.
    length of room
    height of door
    height of closet

Does anything in the room measure 1 km?   1 hm?   1 dam?

What would we measure outside that would be a km or more?
    Part of a highway   Other ideas?
    State border
    Distance to moon

THROUGH THE "ROCKY" MOUNTAINS

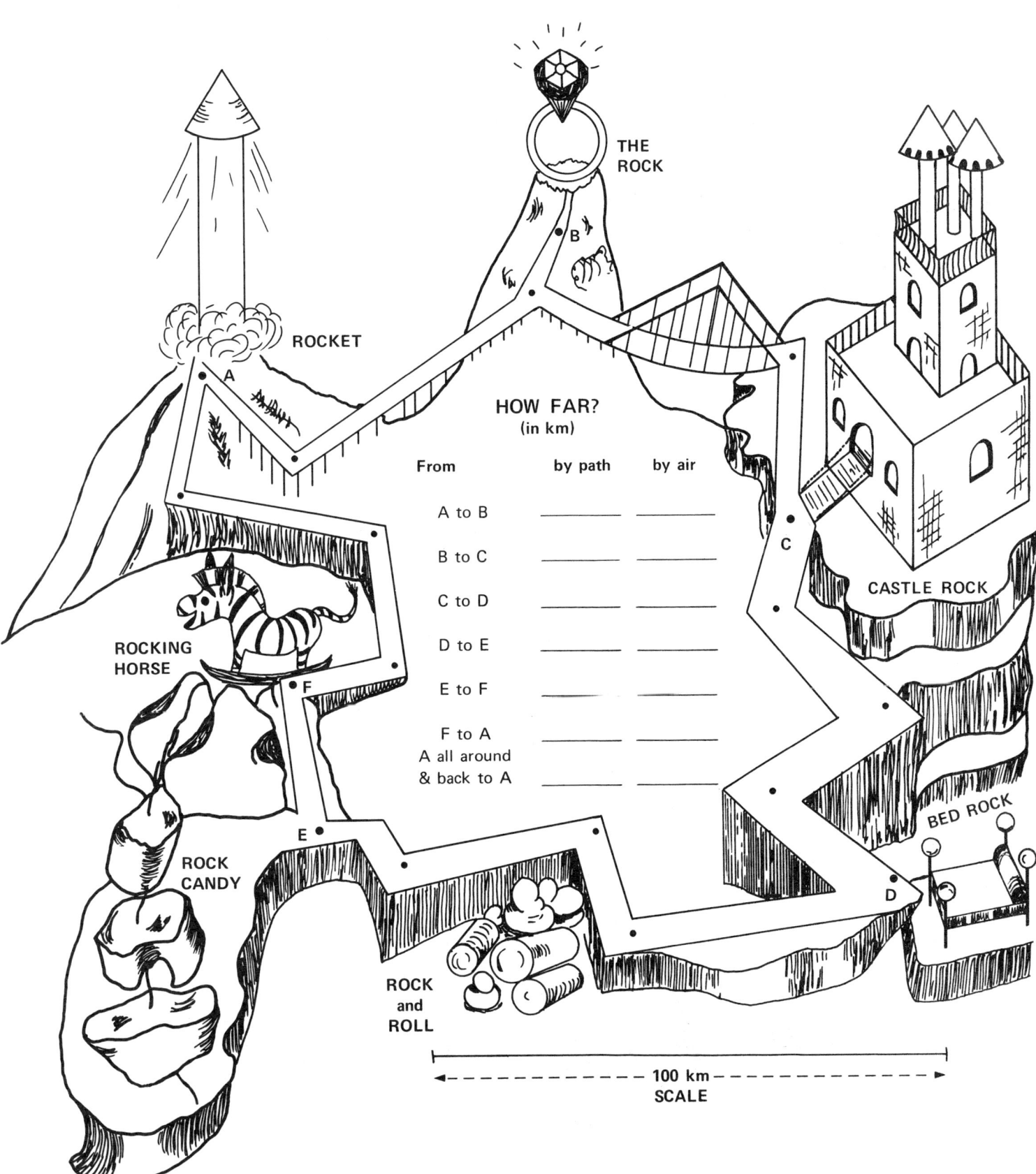

23

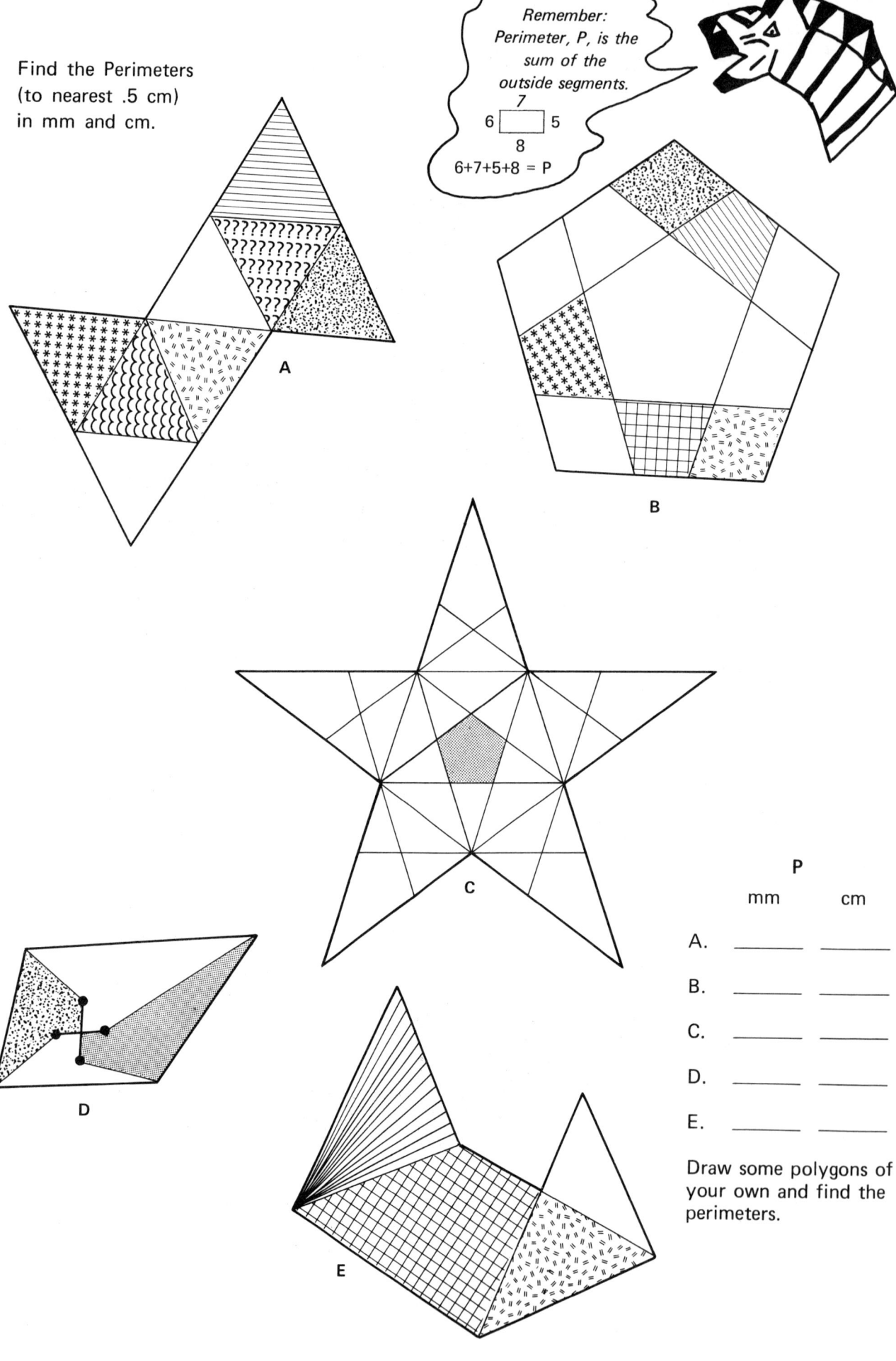

SLIDE METRIC: cm

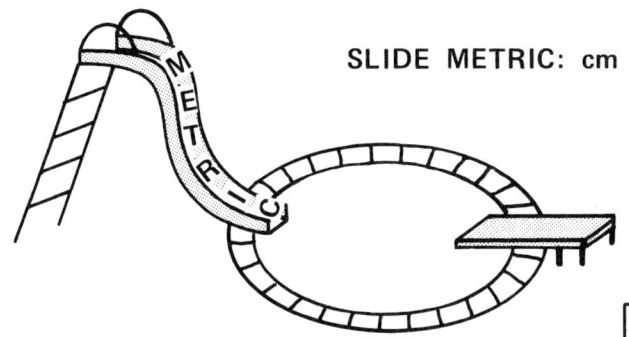

Cut out the two cm number lines below. Fold #2 on dotted line. Slide #1 in fold.

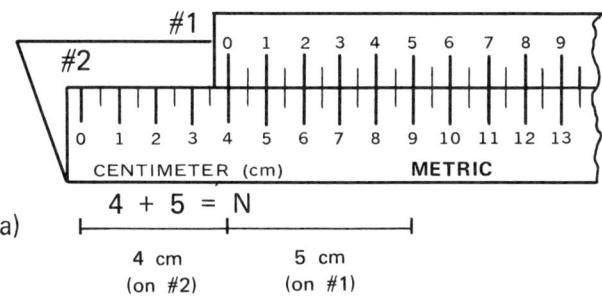

a) $4 + 5 = N$

    4 cm   5 cm
   (on #2)   (on #1)

$N = 9$ (on #2)

b) $9 - 4 = N$

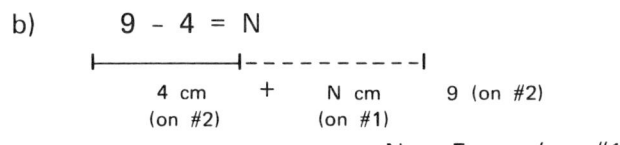

  4 cm + N cm   9 (on #2)
(on #2)   (on #1)

$N = 5$ cm (on #1)

Use Slide Metric

$3 \text{ cm} + 8 \text{ cm} = N$
$N = \underline{\qquad}$

$2 \text{ cm} + 9 \text{ cm} = N$
$N = \underline{\qquad}$

$11 \text{ cm} + 4 \text{ cm} = N$
$N = \underline{\qquad}$

$8.5 \text{ cm} + 6.5 \text{ cm} = N$
$N = \underline{\qquad}$

$6.5 \text{ cm} + 8.5 \text{ cm} = N$
$N = \underline{\qquad}$

$18 \text{ cm} - 11 \text{ cm} = N$
$N = \underline{\qquad}$

$9 \text{ cm} - 3 \text{ cm} = N$
$N = \underline{\qquad}$

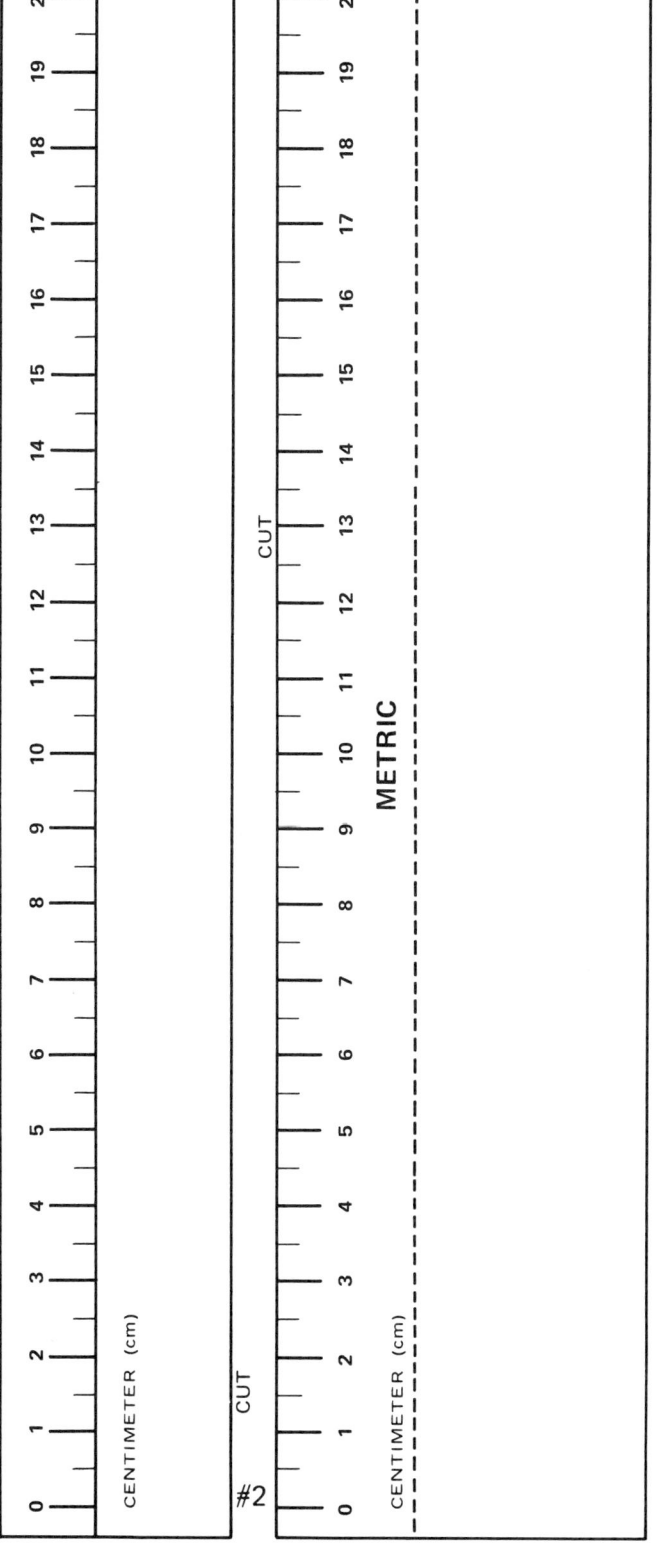

Metric System of Measurement © Activity Resources Co. Hayward, CA 94540

SLIDE METRIC: mm

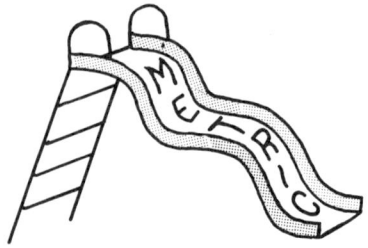

Cut out the two mm number lines below. Fold #2 on dotted line. Slide #1 in fold.

Use Slide Metric

14 mm + 26 mm = N
N = _____

40 mm − 26 mm = N
N = _____

28 mm + 28 mm = N
N = _____

36 mm + 120 mm = N
N = _____

73 mm + 29 mm = N
N = _____

185 mm − 26 mm = N
N = _____

135 mm − 64 mm = N
N = _____

82 mm − 37 mm = N
N = _____

38 mm − 14 mm = N
N = _____

Use #1 from Slide Metric (cm) in the #2 Slide Metric (mm) (or vice versa) to make make a Slide Metric (cm - mm - dm)
1 dm = 10 cm

Compare the two scales:

3 cm = _____ mm

_____ cm = 150 mm

193 mm = _____ dm _____ cm _____ mm

_____ mm = .75 dm

9 cm − 45 mm = _____

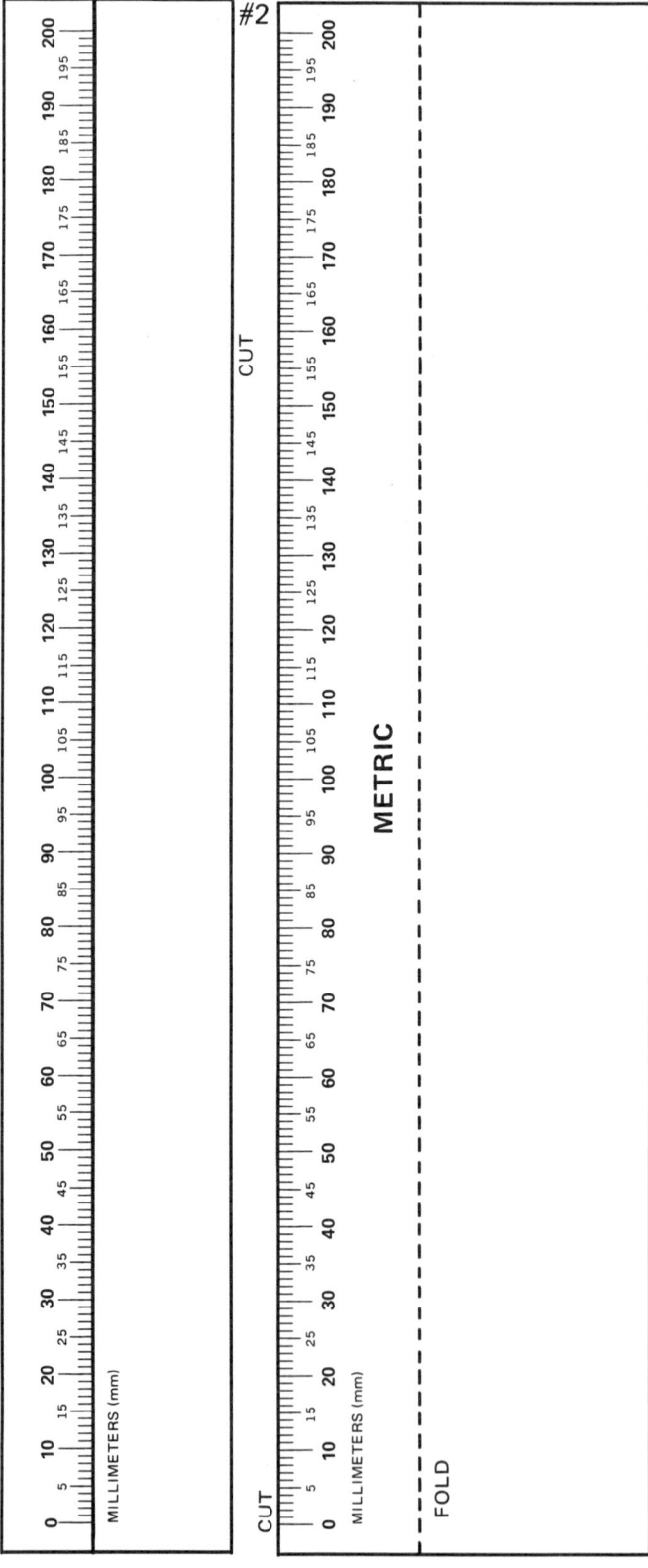

26

Metric System of Measurement © Activity Resources Co. Hayward, CA 94540

IDEAS IN LINEAR MEASUREMENT

with materials probably in your classroom or home.

1. Gather pieces of ribbon, string, lace, yarn, shoelaces . . . What is the measurement of each using mm, cm, dm, and/or m, — whichever is appropriate? Record results in a chart or on a graph.

2. List five or more things in your home that measure, in at least one direction, 1 mm, 1 cm, 1 dm, 1 m.

3. Construct a metric trundle wheel (if one is not available in the classroom).

    Cut a string one meter long — use the meter stick and mark off the ten decimeters with a felt pen.

    Curve the string into a circle on a heavy peice of cardboard. Copy the circle and mark off the 10 dm (a chalkboard compass will help). Place an arrow on one of the dm for the starting point. Cut out circle.

    Run a thin nail through the center of the circle.

    Use as described on page 11 for the little dm wheel.

4. Use a metric tape or metric trundle wheel to measure the painted lines surrounding game locations on the playyard.

basketball court	volley ball court	playing field
hop scotch figure	circle game court	soccer
kickball diamond		baseball

5. Measure a line 50 m long. Using normal strides, walk the line up and back (100 m) counting how many strides. 100 ÷ your count = length of your stride.

6. Use relationship rods that are based on 1 cm^3 and form trains of different lengths. Build towers and find the heights in cm or dm.

    Which rod measures 1 dm? Form a meter with them. How many cm would match it?

    Using rods of 2 cm, 3 cm, 5 cm, and 7 cm only — (you may use any of these more than once), can you make at least one train to match all the numbers from 4-30? Keep a list of any you can't do and check with other students to see if they could make the train.

    | 2 | + | 3 | + | 3 | + | 5 | + | 7 | = 20 |

7. Cut out many large letters from magazines and newspapers.

    Measure their heighths in cm and mm.

    Paste the letters on a background paper to form an attractive pattern.

    Make cartoon figures using some of the letters.

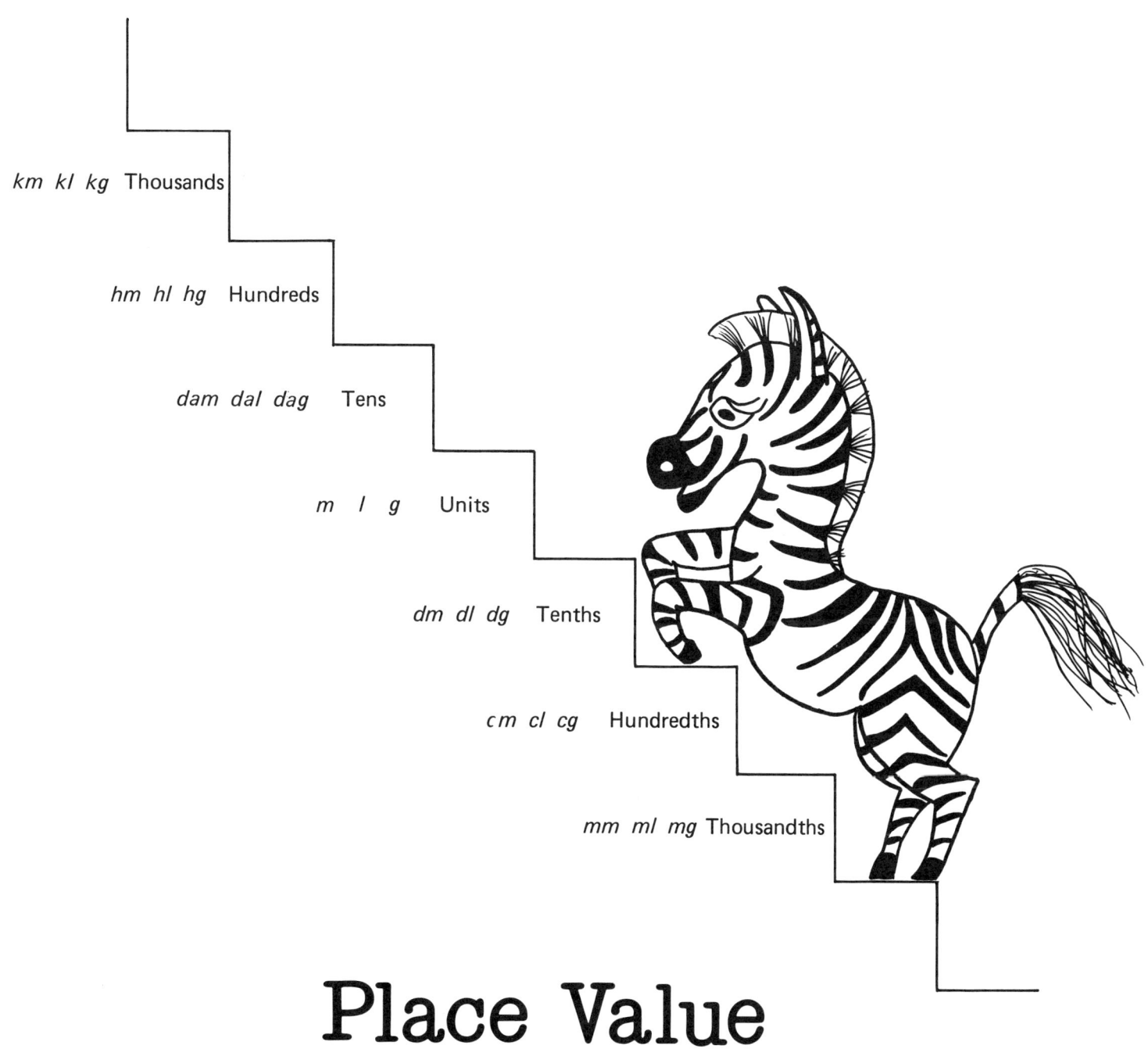

Place Value and Metric

SECTION TWO

BASED ON TEN

Decimal System base ten	Thousands 1000 1000.0	Hundreds 100 100.0	Tens 10 10.0	Units 1	Tenths $\frac{1}{10}$ .1	Hundredths $\frac{1}{100}$ .01	Thousandths $\frac{1}{1000}$ .001
Metric System (SI)* based on ten (prefixes & meanings)	kilo — 1000 k	hecto — 100 h	deka — 10 da	unit of measure 1	deci — .1 d	centi — .01 c	milli — .001 m
Length	kilometer km	hectometer hm	dekameter dam	Meter m	decimeter dm	centimeter cm	millimeter mm
Mass	kilogram kg	hectogram hg	dekagram dag	Gram g	decigram dg	centigram cg	milligram mg
Liquid Capacity	kiloliter kl	hectoliter hl	dekaliter dal	Liter l	deciliter dl	centiliter cl	milliliter ml

Same prefixes but relationship different.

Area Squared	square kilometer km²	square hectometer hm²	square dekameter dam²	Square Meter m²	square decimeter dm²	square centimeter cm²	square millimeter mm²
Volume Cubed	cubic kilometer km³	cubic hectometer hm³	cubic dekameter dam³	Cubic Meter m³	cubic decimeter dm³	cubic centimeter cm³	cubic millimeter mm³
	1,000,000	10,000	100	1 m²	.01	.0001	.000001
	1,000,000,000	1,000,000	1,000	1 m³	.001	.000001	.000000001

*SI — Systems International

BASED ON TEN

10 milli (m/g/l) = 1 centi (m/g/l)

10 centi (m/g/l) = 1 deci (m/g/l)

10 deci (m/g/l) = 1 (m/g/l)

10 (m/g/l) = 1 deka (m/g/l)

10 deka (m/g/l) = 1 hecto (m/g/l)

10 hecto (m/g/l) = 1 kilo (m/g/l)

1000 milli —
100 centi —   } = 1 (m/g/l)
10 deci —

100 deka —
10 hecto —   } = 1000 (m/g/l)
1 kilo —

Use the "Based on Ten" chart

a) In the top chart as you move from any position to the position

1 to the right you _____ by <u>ten:</u> ; 1 to the left you _____ by <u>ten</u>

2 to the right you _____ by _____ ; 2 to the left you _____ by _____

3 to the right you _____ by _____ ; 3 to the left you _____ by _____

b) If 1 km = 1000 m, then 1 kg = _____ g and
                           1 kl = _____ l.

c) If .001 ($\frac{1}{1000}$) of a m = 1 mm then _____ of a g = 1 mg and
                                                 _____ of a l = 1 ml

d) Which metric unit — m, g, l, m^2, m^3, — would be used to measure:

how heavy _____   how much gasoline _____

how tall _____   frame for picture _____

how much water _____   gravel in a truck _____

rug for floor _____   butter _____

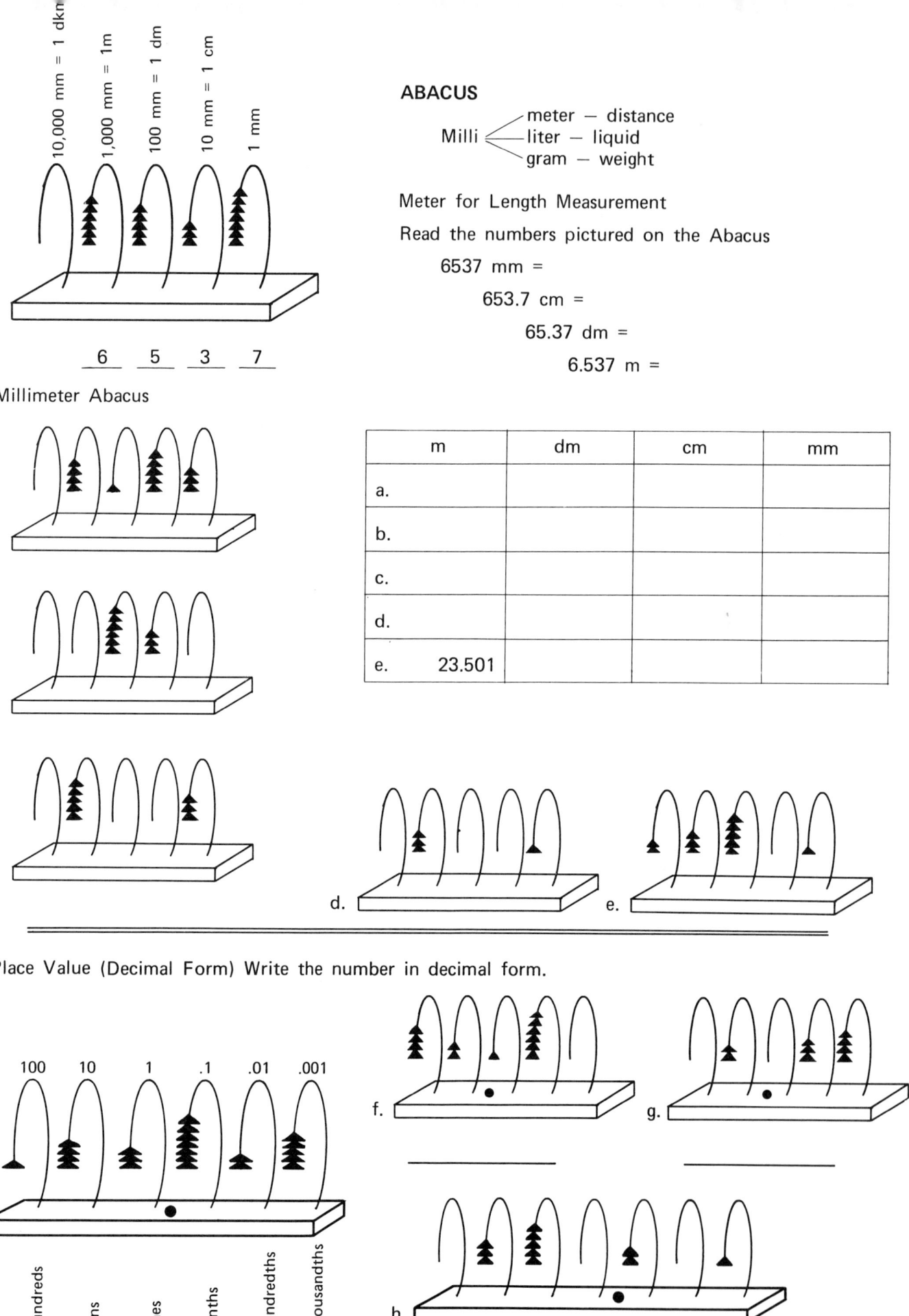

LITER (l)

To measure liquid capacity:

A milliliter abacus

(a)

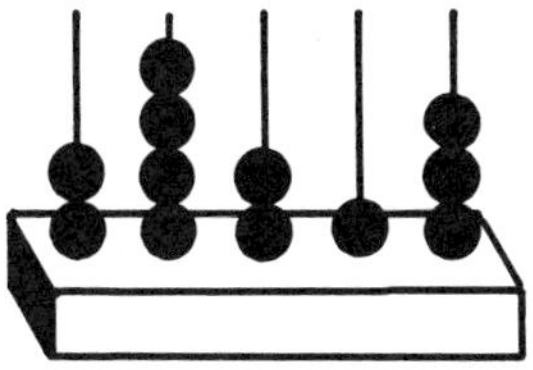

l dl cl ml

Record the measures that you read from the abacus in this chart in —

	l	*dl*	*cl*	*ml*
(a)	24.213			
(b)			305.2	
(c)				
(d)				
(e)				

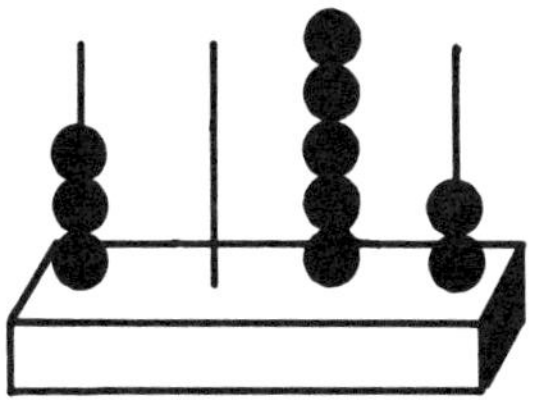

(b) 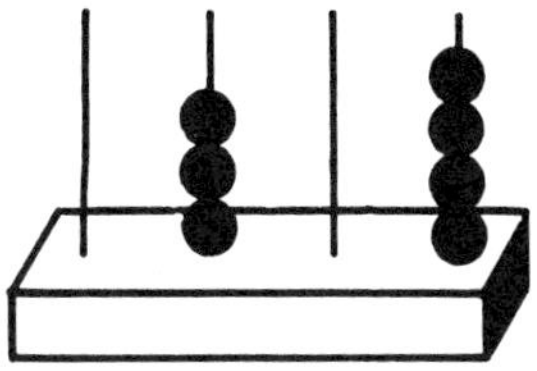   (c)

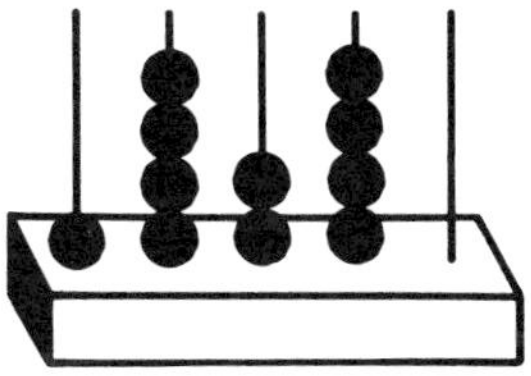

(d) 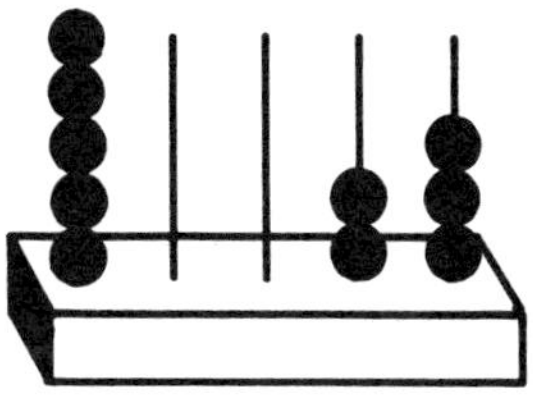   (e)

GRAM (g)

To measure weight —

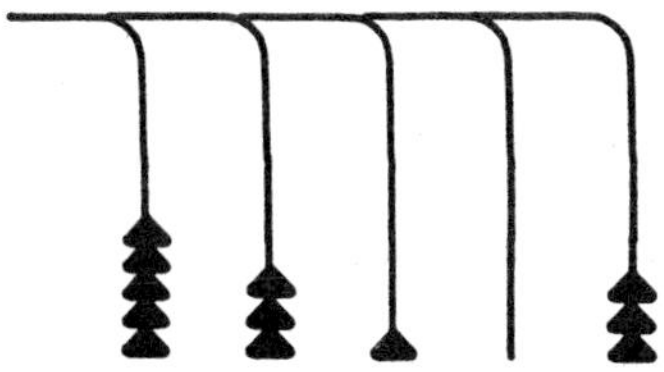

Milligram abacus

(f) 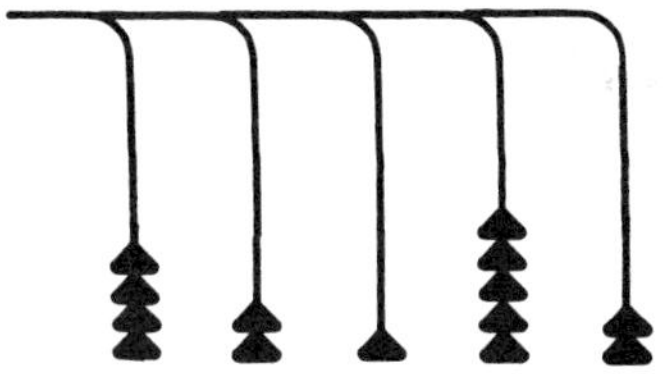 *g dg cg mg*   (g)   (h) 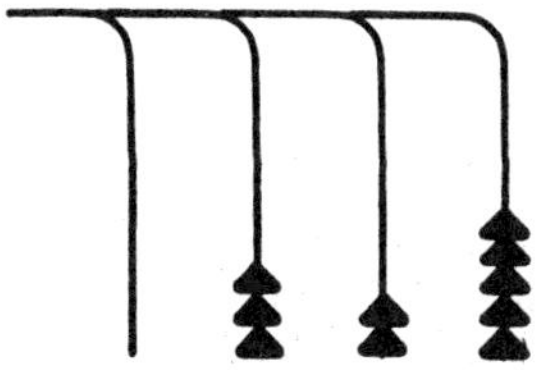   (i)

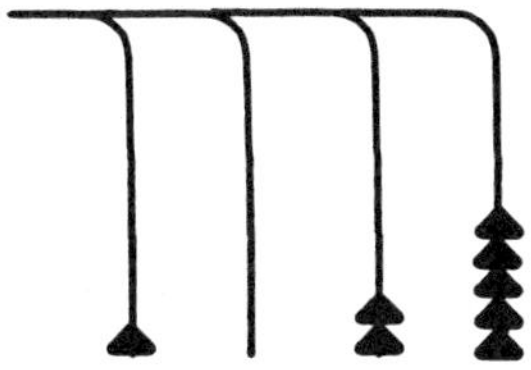

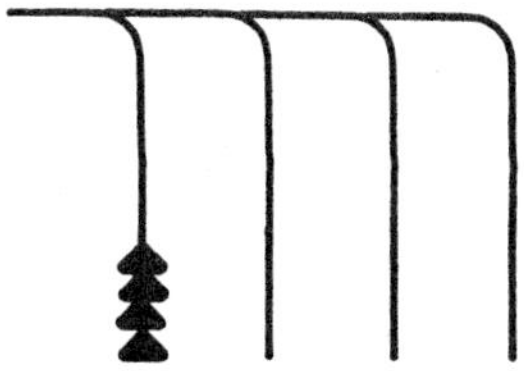

(j)

	g	*dg*	*cg*	*mg*
(f)	42.152			
(g)				
(h)				
(i)				
(j)				

A JUST SUPPOSE MONEY SYSTEM

1 millidollar (m$)  = .001$

1 centidollar (c$)  = .01$

1 decidollar (d$)  = .1$

1 Dollar($)  = 1$

1 dekadollar (da$)  = 10$

1 hectodollar (h$)  = 100$

1 kilodollar (k$)  = 1000$

a)

_____ m$ = 1 c$
_____ m$ = 1 d$
_____ m$ = 1$
_____ c$ = 1 d$
_____ c$ = 1$
_____ $ = 1 k$

b)

4 $ = _____ c$
25 $ = _____ d$
8 $ = _____ m$
135 $ = _____ c$

c)

_____ da $ = 8 $
_____ h $ = 270 $
_____ k $ = 5200 $
_____ $ = 9 d$
_____ h $ = 2400 c$
_____ k $ = 43 h$

d)

27 k$ = _____ da$
5 da$ = _____ d$
345 h$ = _____ c$

═══

Working with dollars, dimes & pennies.

e) 147 pennies = $ _____   f) $2.48 = _____ pennies
    328 dimes = $ _____ $53.40 = _____ dimes
    16 dimes & 8 pennies = $ _____ $.28 = _____ pennies
    4 dollars and 3 pennies = $ _____ $157.38 = _____ pennies
    4 dimes = $ _____ $520.90 = _____ dimes
    7 pennies = $ _____

34

Metric System of Measurement © Activity Resources Co. Hayward, CA 94540

RELATION TO THE WHOLE
Picturing Metric Measurements

If the entire square represents:

(A) one whole, then the measure of

		Fraction	Decimal
□	is	$\frac{1}{100}$	.01
(5×10 grid)	is		.50
(1×10 strip)	is	$\frac{10}{100}$	
(shape)	is		
(shape)	is		
(shape)	is		
TOTAL			1.00

(Use decimal form in this chart.)

If the entire square represents:		□	(5×10)	(1×10)	(shape)	(shape)	(shape)	TOTAL	PREFIX
(B)	ONE METER	1 cm		10 cm				cm	centi
		dm	5 dm					dm	
		.01 m				.14 m		m	✕
(C)	ONE GRAM	cg			20 cg			cg	
		1 dg						dg	
		g	.5 g						✕
(D)	ONE LITER	1 cl	50 cl					cl	
		dl						dl	
		l			.05 l			l	✕
* (E)	ONE SQUARE METER	cm²	5000 cm²		2000 cm²			10,000 cm²	
		1 dm²				5 dm²	14 dm²	100 dm²	
		.01 m²	.5 m²	.1 m²				1 m²	✕
* (F)	ONE SQUARE DECIMETER	100 mm²		1000 mm²	500 mm²			10,000 mm²	
		1 cm²	50 cm²		20 cm²			100 cm²	
		dm²		.1 cm²			.14 dm²	1 dm²	deci

*Only for those who care to square.

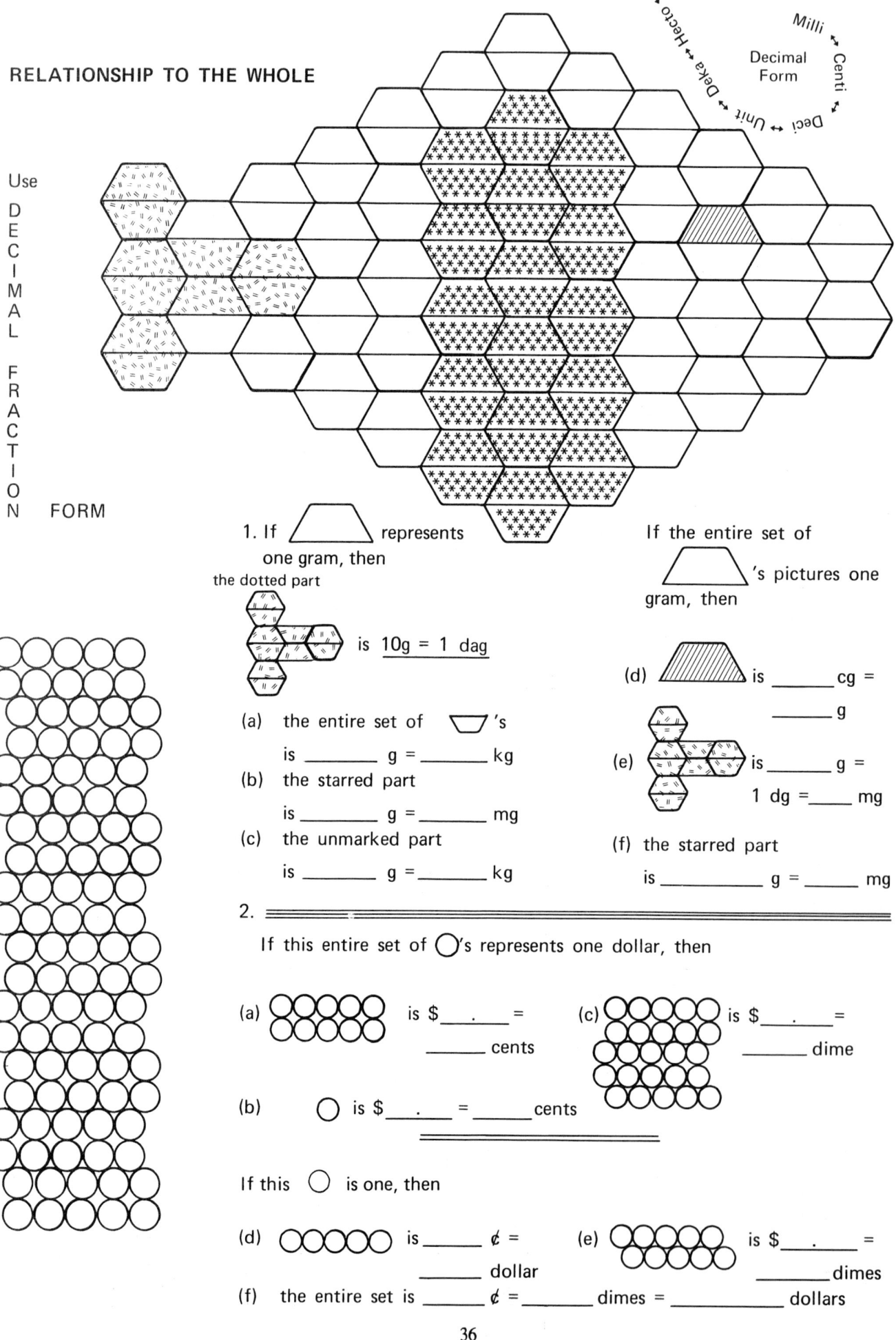

RELATIONSHIP TO THE WHOLE

Decimal Form

Use decimal form

1. If the entire set of ⬡'s represents one deciliter (dl), then
   a) the shaded ⬢ part is _____ dl = _____ ml
   b) the ⊗ is _____ dl = _____ cl
   c) the ? part is _____ cl = _____ l
   d) the /// part is _____ ml = _____ l

   If ⊗ represents one liter, then
   e) the /// part is _____ l = _____ ml
   f) the ? part is _____ kl = _____ l
   g) the clear part is _____ l = _____ cl
   h) the shaded part is _____ kl = _____ ml
   i) the entire set is _____ l = _____ kl

2. If △ represents one meter, then
   a) the ═ part is _____ m = _____ km
   and the entire figure is _____ m = 1

   If △ represents one millimeter, then
   b) the ═ part is _____ mm = 1 _____
   c) and the entire figure is _____ mm = 1 _____

   If the entire figure represents one kilometer, then
   d) the △ is _____ km = _____ m
   e) and the ≡ is _____ km = 1 _____
   f) and the clear part is _____ km = _____ m

X and ÷ by 10, 10 x 10, 10 x 10 x 10

If the large square is one hundred, then

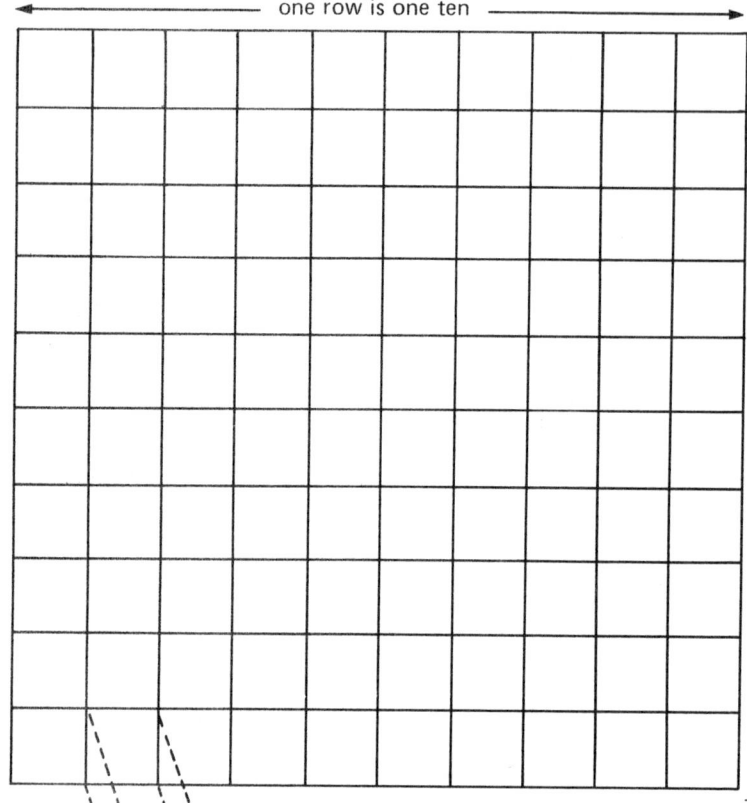

If	Then
2 x 10 = 20,	20 ÷ 10 = 2
3 x 10 = 30,	30 ÷ 10 = 3
4 x 10 = 40,	40 ÷ 10 = 4
5 x 10 = 50,	50 ÷ 10 = 5
6 x 10 = 60,	60 ÷ 10 = 6
7 x 10 = 70,	70 ÷ 10 = 7
8 x 10 = 80,	80 ÷ 10 = 8
9 x 10 = 90,	90 ÷ 10 = 9
10 x 10 = 100,	100 ÷ 10 = 10

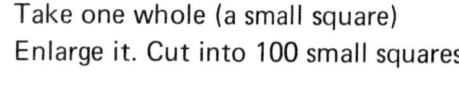

Take one whole (a small square)
Enlarge it. Cut into 100 small squares

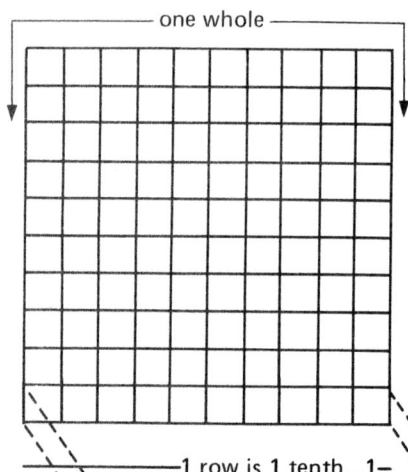

If	Then
.1 x 10 = 1,	1 ÷ 10 = .1
.3 x 10 = 3,	3 ÷ 10 = .3
.7 x 10 = ____,	____ ÷ 10 = ____
2.5 x 10 = ____,	____ ÷ 10 = ____
.4 x 10 x 10 = ____,	____ ÷ 100 = ____
8.9 x 100 = ____,	____ ÷ 100 = ____
6.3 x 1000 = ____,	____ ÷ 1000 = ____

Take one of these rows, .1, and ⟶

X AND ÷ BY 10, 100, 1000 (Con't)

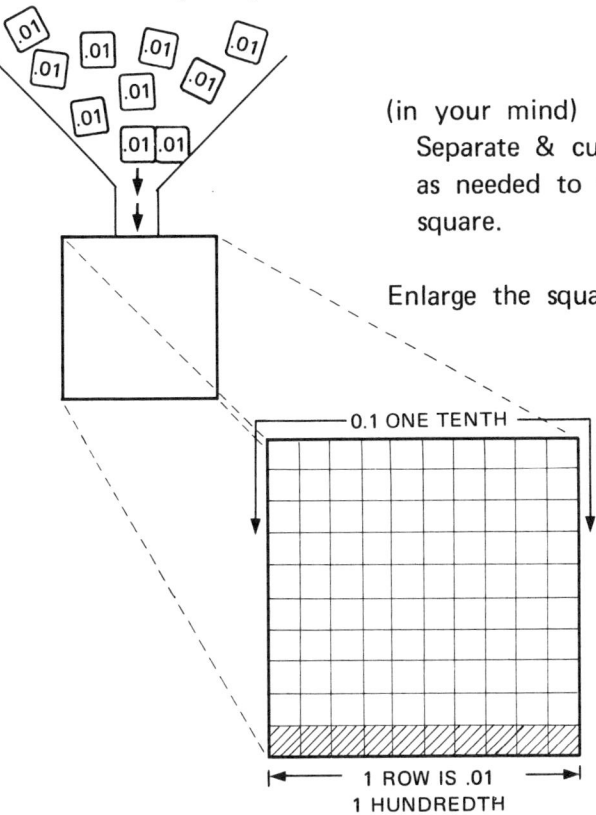

(in your mind)
Separate & cut the parts as needed to form a square.

Enlarge the square.

a) If   Then

.01 × 10 = .1 , .1 ÷ 10 = .01
.08 × 10 = .8 , .8 ÷ 10 = .08
.19 × 10 = ____ , ____ ÷ 10 = ____
6.03 × 10 = ____ , ____ ÷ 10 = ____
.56 × 100 = ____ , ____ ÷ 100 = ____
2.43 × 1000 = ____ , ____ ÷ 1000 = ____

b) If   Then

11 × 10 = ____ , 110 ÷ 10 = ____
12 × 10 = ____ , ____ ÷ 10 = ____
19 × 10 = ____ , ____ ÷ 10 = ____
379 × 10 = ____ , ____ ÷ 10 = ____
849 × 10 = ____ , ____ ÷ 10 = ____

If (100 = 10 × 10) Then (1000 = 10 × 10 × 10))

47 × 10 × 10 = ____ , ____ ÷ 100 = ____
59 × 10 × 10 = ____ , ____ ÷ 100 = ____
97 × 10 × 10 × 10 = ____ , ____ ÷ 1000 = ____
256 × 1000 = ____ , ____ ÷ 1000 = ____
.5 × 100 = ____ , ____ ÷ 100 = ____

c) 38.6 × 1000 = ____
25.70 ÷ 10 = ____
1305 ÷ 100 = ____
48 × 100 = ____
29 ÷ 10 = ____
4.91 ÷ 100 = ____
.65 × 1000 = ____
.013 ÷ 10 = ____
.002 × 100 = ____
1.47 × 10 = ____

EXPONENTS — A shorter way to write a number.

$2^4 = 2 \times 2 \times 2 \times 2 = 16$
base two to the fourth power is sixteen

②^4 is the *base*
$2$④ is the *exponent*
②④ is the *power of the base*

$3^5 = 3 \times 3 \times 3 \times 3 \times 3 = 243$
three to the fifth power is 243

$5^2 = $ _____ × _____ = _____ $1^7 =$

$8^3 = $ $9^3 =$

$6^4 = $ $3^1 =$

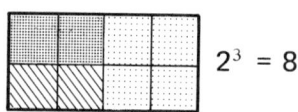
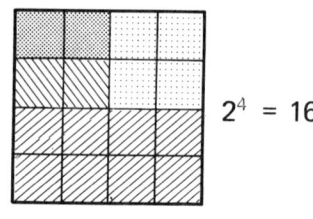

$2^0 = 1$
$2^1 = 2$
$2^2 = 4$
$2^3 = 8$
$2^4 = 16$

Decimal (base ten) System

Ten Thousands	Thousands	Hundreds	Tens	Units	
10×10×10×10	10×10×10	10×10	10	1	Exponent Form
10^4	10^3	10^2	10^1	10^0	
10,000	1,000	100	10	1	

Expanded notation:

      $3 = 3 \times 1$
     $50 = 5 \times 10 - 5 \times 10^1$
    $400 = 5 \times 10 \times 10 = 4 \times 10^2$
+ $6000 = 6 \times 10 \times 10 \times 10 = 6 \times 10^3$

   $6453 = (6 \times 10^3) + (4 \times 10^2) + (5 \times 10^1) + (3 \times 10^0)$

$5,020,075 = (5 \times \underline{\quad}) + (2 \times \underline{\quad}) + (7 \times \underline{\quad}) + (5 \times \underline{\quad})$
$807 =$
$900,200 =$
_____ $= (7 \times 10^5) + (3 \times 10^4) + (2 \times 10^2) + (7 \times 10^0)$
_____ $= (1 \times 10^3) + (2 \times 10^2) + (8 \times 10^1)$
_____ $= (9 \times 10^1) + (3 \times 10^3) + (8 \times 10^0) + (5 \times 10^5)$

USING EXPONENTS IN THE DECIMAL (BASE TEN) SYSTEM

100 x 1000 = 100,000	100,000 ÷ 1000 = 100	1000 x 1 = 1000
10^2 x 10^3 = 10^5	10^5 ÷ 10^3 = 10^2	10^3 x 10^0 = 10^3
1000 x 10,000 = 10,000,000	10,000,000 ÷ 10,000 = 1,000	100 ÷ 1 = 10^0
10^3 x 10^4 = 10^7	10^7 ÷ 10^4 = 10^3	10^2 ÷ 10^0 = 10^2
to x add exponents if base is same	observe the exponents / to ÷ subtract exponents if base is the same	

10^1 x 10^1 = 10^7 ÷ 10^1 = 10^5 x 10^2 =

10^6 x 10^0 = 10^3 ÷ 10^0 = 10^0 x 10^0 =

10^3 x 10^3 = 10^4 ÷ 10^2 = 10^2 ÷ 10^1 =

10^8 ÷ 10^7 = 10^3 x 10^2 = 10^6 ÷ 10^3 =

10^3 ÷ 10^3 = 10^1 x 10^3 = 10^3 ÷ 10^1 =

$\dfrac{10^3}{10^2}=$ $\dfrac{10^5}{10^5}=$ $\dfrac{10^5}{10^4}=$

ONLY FOR EXPERTS

Extending Exponents

Millions	Hundred Thousands	Ten Thousds	Thousands	Hundreds	Tens	Unit	Tenths	Hundredths	Thousandths	Ten Thousandths
1,000,000	100,000	10,000	1,000	100	10	1	$\frac{1}{10}=.1$	$\frac{1}{1000}=.01$	$\frac{1}{1000}=.001$	$\frac{1}{10,000}=.0001$
10^6	10^5	10^4	10^3	10^2	10^1	10^0	10^{-1}	10^{-2}	10^{-3}	10^{-4}

$23.46 = (2 \times 10^1) + (3 \times 10^0) + (4 \times 10^{-1}) + (6 \times 10^2)$

$.513 =$

_____ $= (5 \times 10^3) + (6 \times 10^0) + (4 \times 10^{-2})$

_____ $= (4 \times 10^2) + (3 \times 10^1) + (1 \times 10^{-1}) + (9 \times 10^{-3})$

10^{-1} x 10^{-3} = _____ 10^5 ÷ 10^6 = _____ 10^1 ÷ 10^{-1} = _____

10^0 x 10^{-2} = _____ 10^0 ÷ 10^3 = _____ 10^2 ÷ 10^6 = _____

10^3 x 10^{-2} = _____ 10^{-1} ÷ 10^{-2} = _____ 10^{-4} x 10^2 = _____

EXPONENTS & SLIDE RULE
x and ÷ on the CD Scales of the Slide Rule.

Cut out CD slides fold #2 and
   insert #1

Use as + and − Slide Metrics since the
   distances represent exponents of ten
      + exponents of ten to x
      − exponents of ten to ÷
(You can use the 1 at either end of
   either slide.)

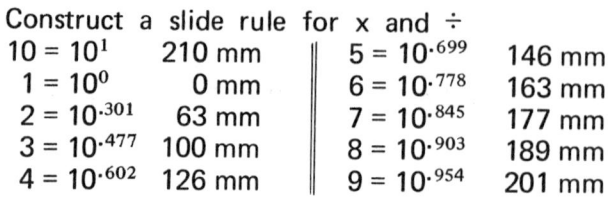

Construct a slide rule for x and ÷

$10 = 10^{1}$	210 mm		$5 = 10^{.699}$	146 mm
$1 = 10^{0}$	0 mm		$6 = 10^{.778}$	163 mm
$2 = 10^{.301}$	63 mm		$7 = 10^{.845}$	177 mm
$3 = 10^{.477}$	100 mm		$8 = 10^{.903}$	189 mm
$4 = 10^{.602}$	126 mm		$9 = 10^{.954}$	201 mm

Try these problems

1 cm x 1 cm = ____1____ cm²

4 x 2 = _____ cm²

3 x 3 = _____ cm²

5 x 2 = _____

8 x 9 = _____

6 x 6 = _____

7 x 8 = _____

21 x 3 = _____

4 x 16 = _____

32 x 3 = _____

27 x 5 = _____

1.5 x 6 = _____

2.5 x 7 = _____

75 x .2 = _____

20 x 18 = _____

16 x 30 = _____

9 ÷ 3 = _____

10 ÷ 5 = _____

6 ÷ 2 = _____

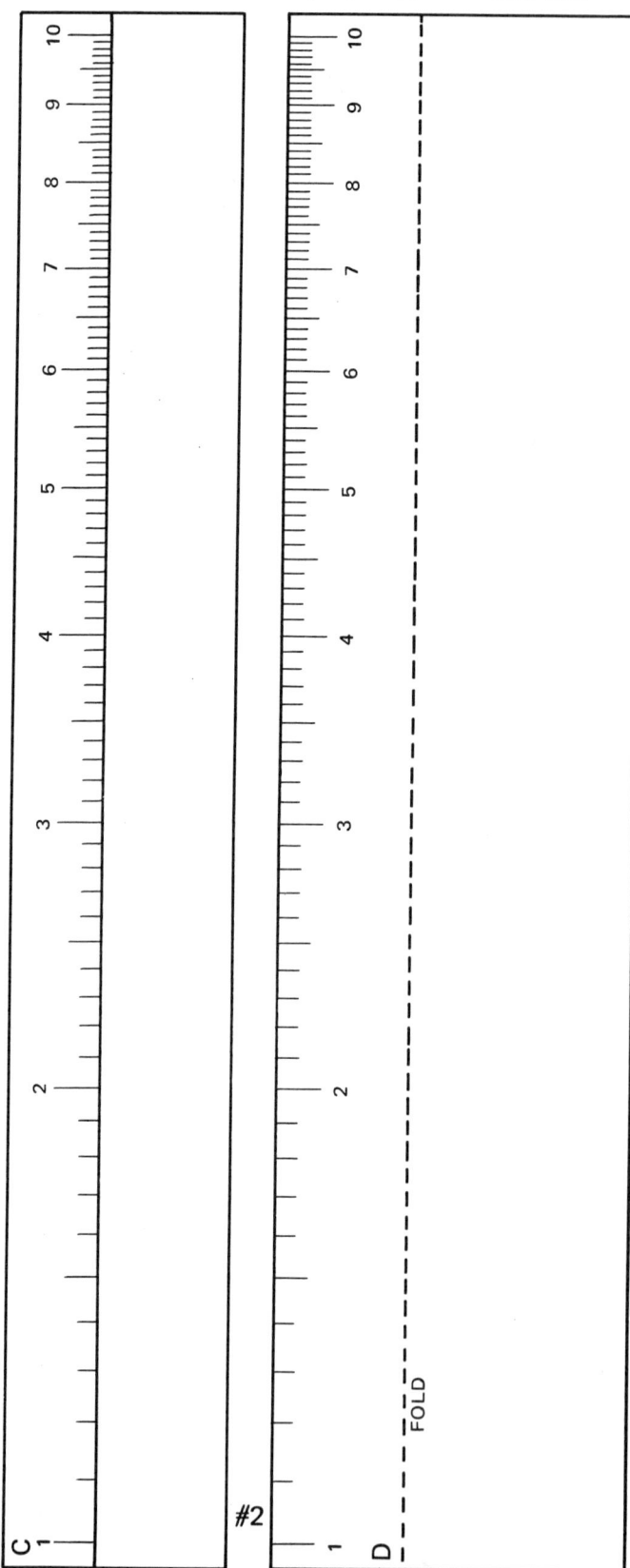

42

Metric System of Measurement © Activity Resources Co. Hayward, CA 94540

Metric Area Measurement

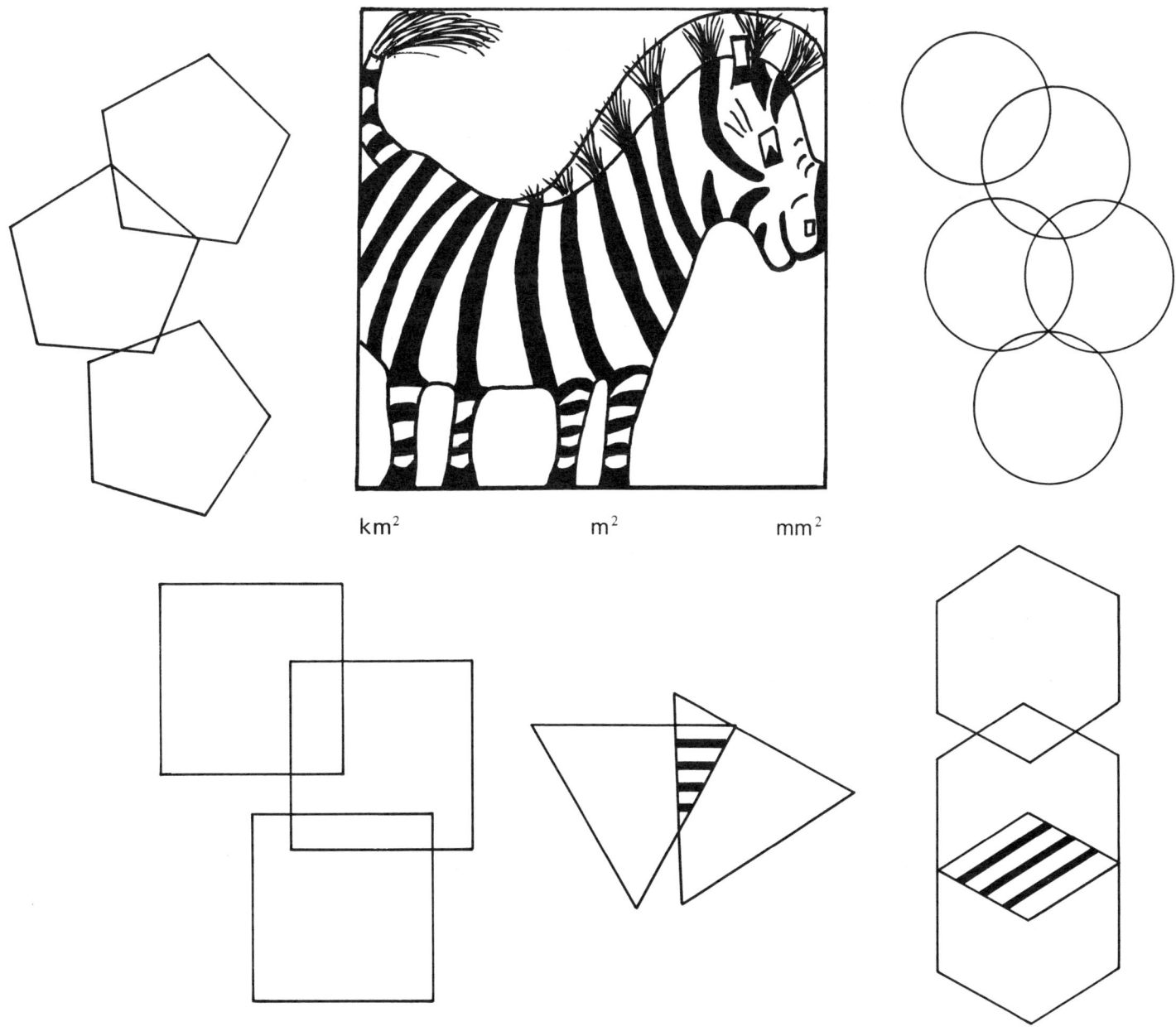

km²   m²   mm²

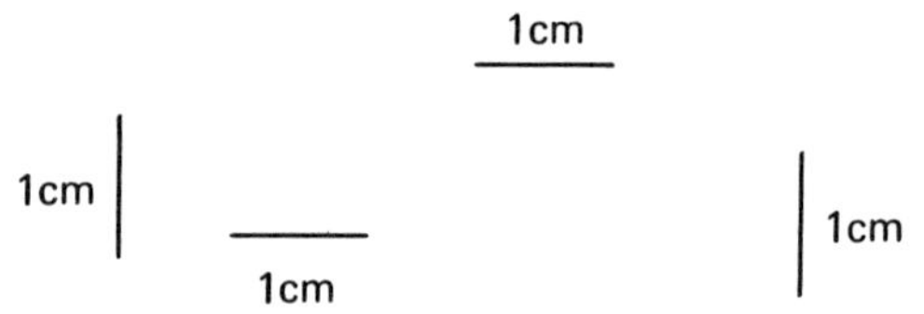

1cm
1cm
1cm
1cm

cm^2 – THE AREA

1cm

1cm by 1cm is $1cm^2$
the Area

Put together, side-by-side, 2 cm^2, $3cm^2$, $4cm^2$, and $5cm^2$

a. Use only 2 – only one shape possible

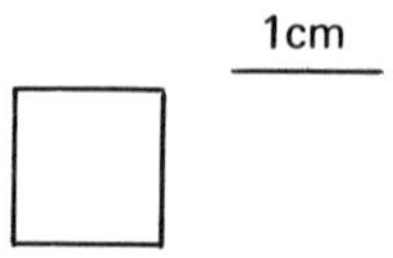

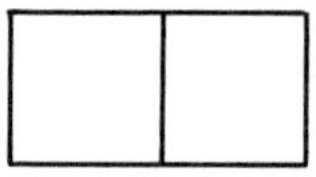

2 cm^2 is the area.

b. Use only 3 – only two different shapes possible.

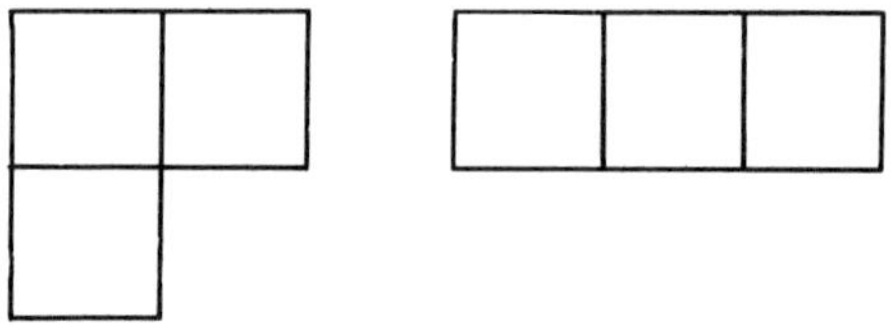

Area = 3 cm^2 each

c. With 4 – only five different shapes.

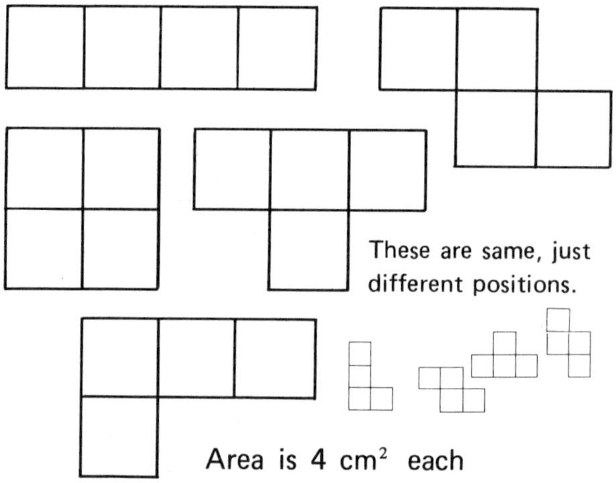

These are same, just different positions.

Area is 4 cm^2 each

d. With 5 – shade in on this grid of $1dm^2$ as many different shapes as you can find.

How many cm^2 in $1dm^2$?

____

Did you find twelve?

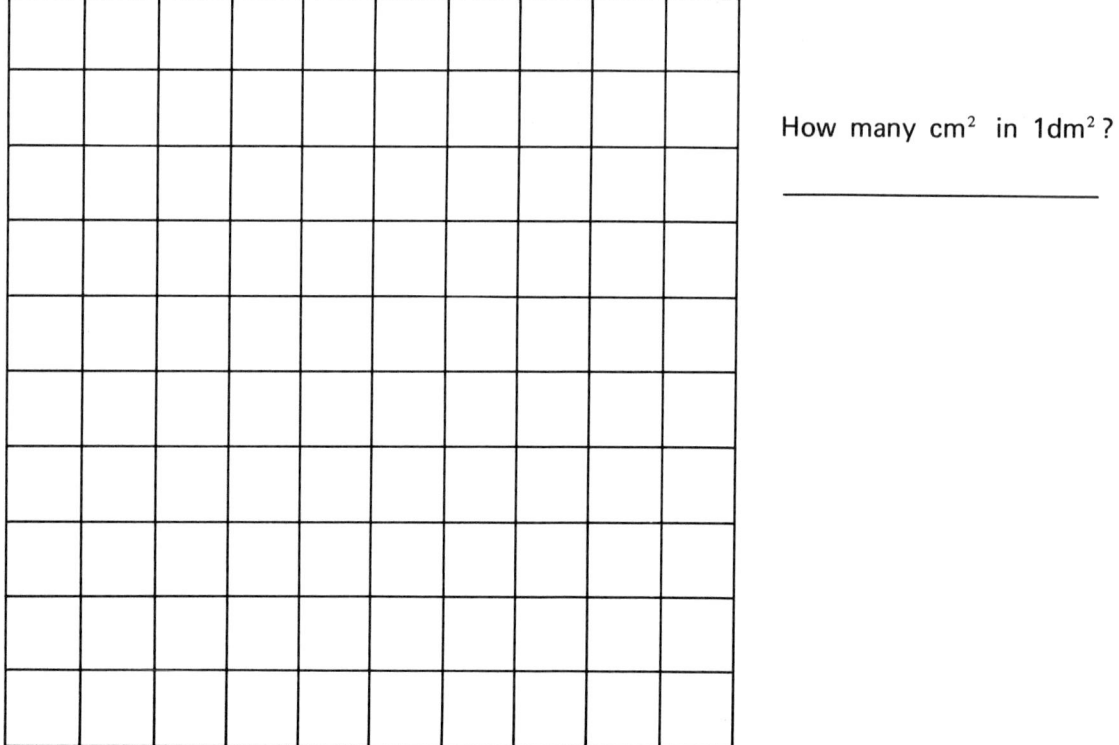

PLOT THE SQUARE NUMBERS

A square number using cm²:

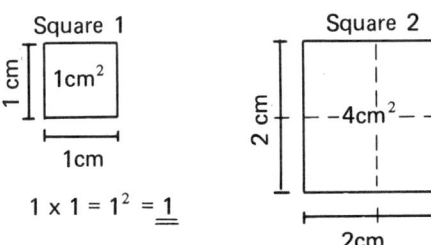

$1 \times 1 = 1^2 = \underline{1}$

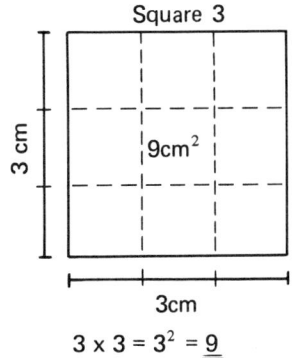

$2 \times 2 = 2^2 = \underline{4}$

Square 3

$3 \times 3 = 3^2 = \underline{9}$

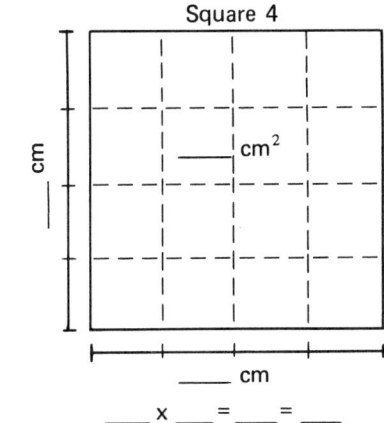

___ × ___ = ___ = ___

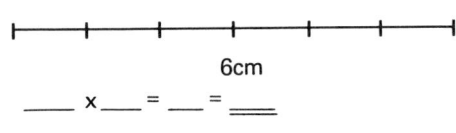

5cm

___ × ___ = ___ = ___

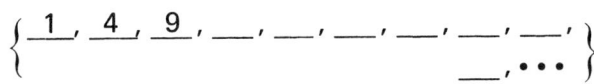

6cm

___ × ___ = ___ = ___

The square numbers are

$\{\underline{1}, \underline{4}, \underline{9}, \underline{}, \underline{}, \underline{}, \underline{}, \underline{}, \underline{}, \underline{}, \ldots\}$

Plot the square No. always using pt. A. Difference between is the square no.

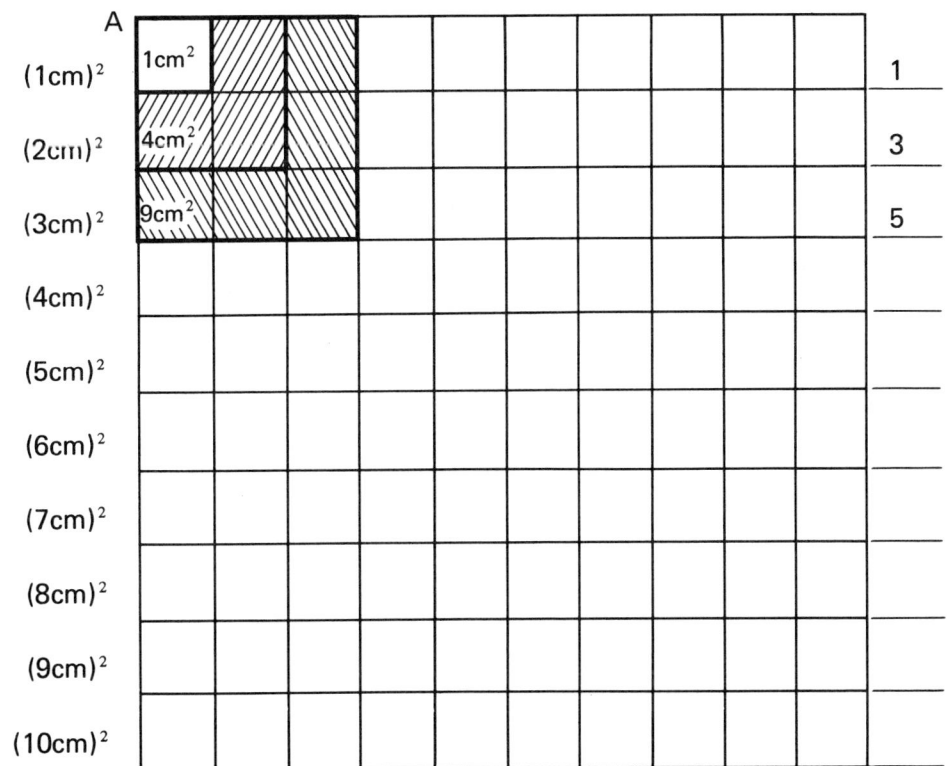

The difference between the square numbers is the

_____ numbers.

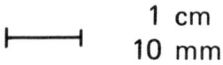 1 mm

├──┤ 1 cm
  10 mm

□ 1 cm²
  1 sq. cm

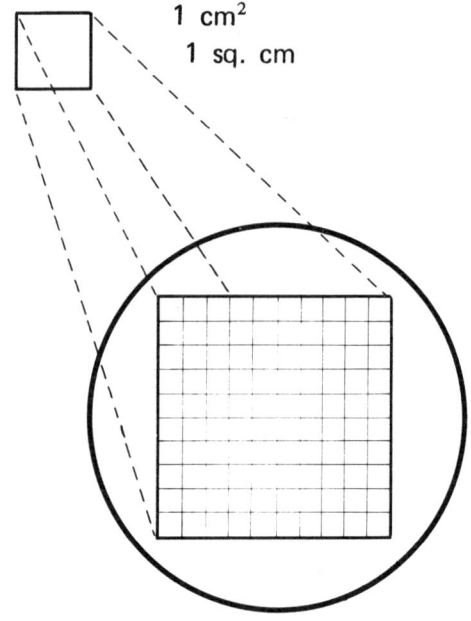

Use a Lens on the 1 cm² 'cause the mm² is itsy-bitsy

1 cm² (sq. cm) = _____ mm² (sq. mm)
200 mm² = 2 cm²

3 cm² = _____ mm²
9 cm² = _____ mm²
15 cm² = _____ mm²
21 cm² = _____ mm²

600 mm² = _____ cm²
1800 mm² = _____ cm²
4700 mm² = _____ cm²
2900 mm² = _____ cm²

150 mm² = __1.50__ cm²
240 mm² = _____ cm²
370 mm² = _____ cm²
1532 mm² = _____ cm²

3.60 cm² = __360__ mm²
7.20 cm² = _____ mm²
14.35 cm² = _____ mm²
90.07 cm² = _____ mm²

46
Metric System of Measurement © Activity Resources Co. Hayward, CA 94540

Connect dots to form more polygons.
Figure the perimeters and areas of the figures. (use mm ruler on diagonals for nearest mm)

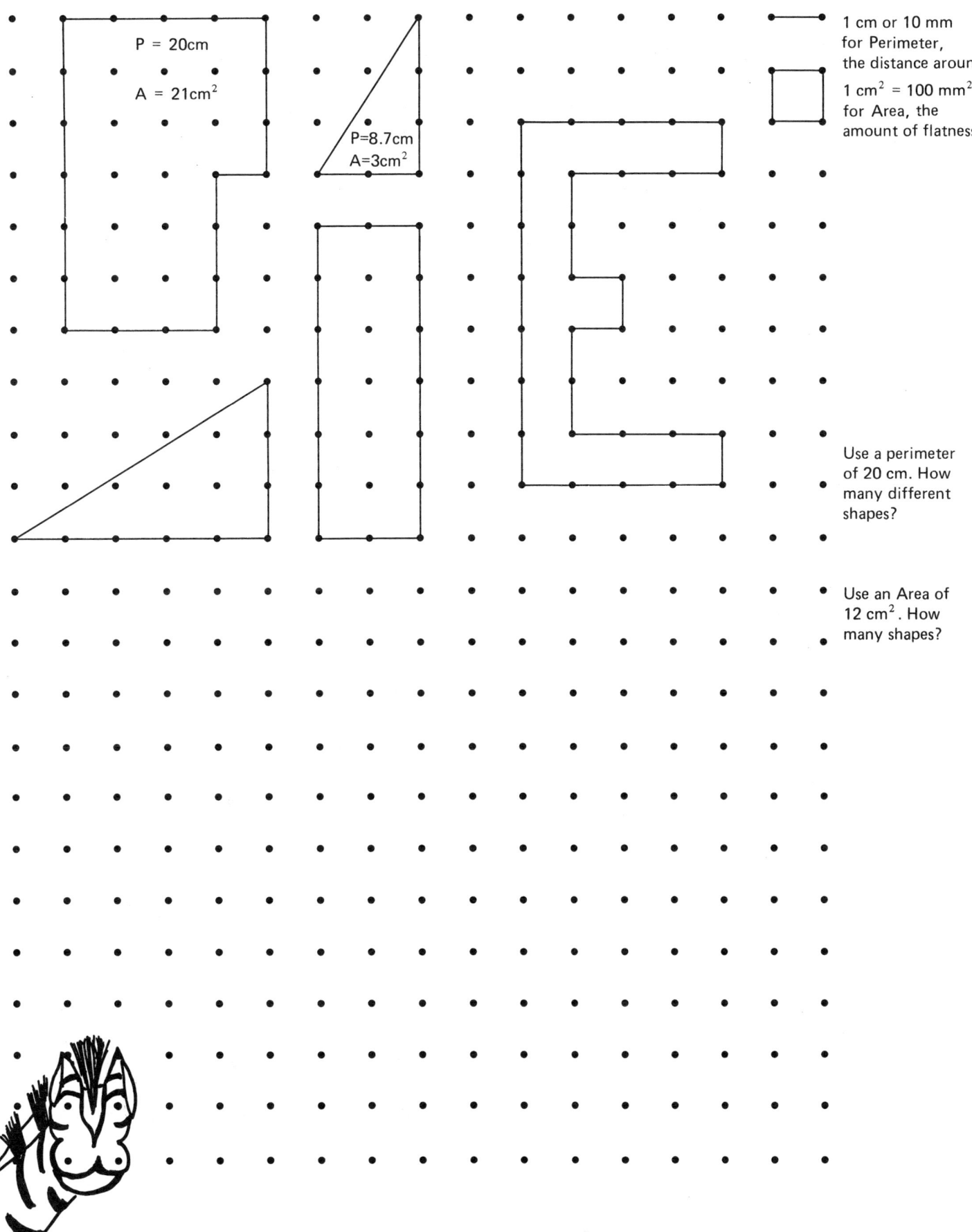

GEOBOARD METRIC

Cut a board 27.5 cm by 27.5 cm and sandpaper for smoothness. Paint if desired.

Place a piece of cm grid paper (27.5 x 27.5) over the face of the board. Arrange the paper so that there is a 1.25 cm margin all around the four sides.

Use 2-cm nails*, 121 in all, pound in 11 nails across at points of intersection every 2.5 cm. Continue for 11 rows every 2.5 cm. You will form 100 squares that are 2.5 cm by 2.5 cm. A washer with a thickness of 1 cm held around the nail when hammering (be careful) will stop the downward progress of the nail when the nailhead touches it. Remove the washer and use on next nail. This allows for uniform height of the nails. Remove grid paper.

Keeping the 1.25 margin on all four sides allows the possibility of using two or more geoboards together side by side.

A smaller geoboard can be made by using squares of 2 cm by 2 cm or a larger board by using 3 cm by 3 cm. The margin would be ½ the cm measure.

*(¾ inch nail in store)

Nails 2.5 cm apart

You will need lots of rubber bands of varying sizes, lengths and colors.

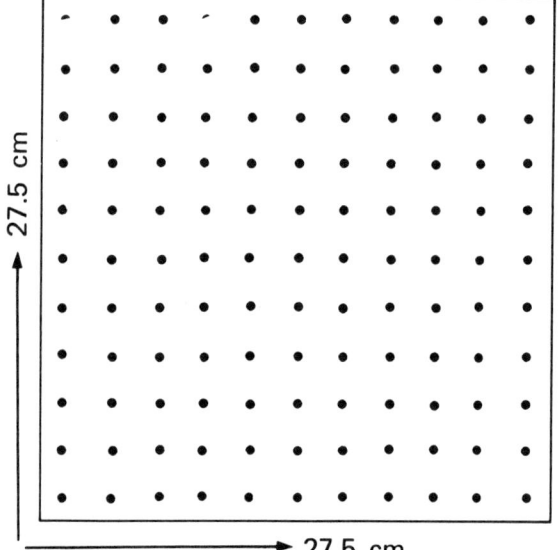

METRIC GEOBOARD
100 squares 2.5 cm x 2.5 cm

1.25 cm margin on all 4 sides

cm grid for placing nails

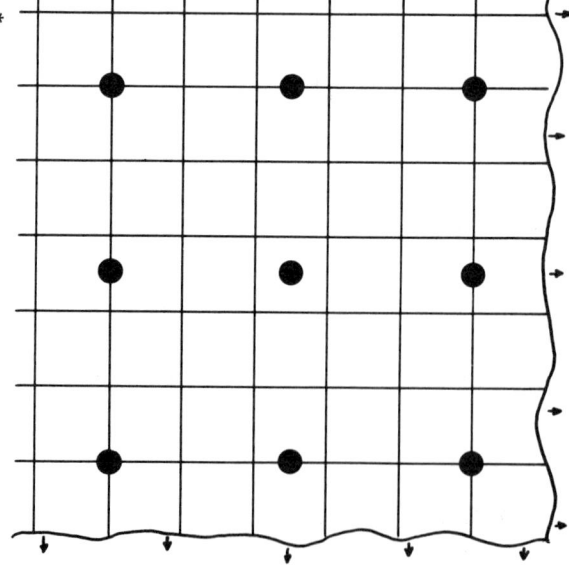

ACTIVITIES ON THE METRIC GEOBOARD

1. On the geoboard use rubber bands to form rectangles, squares, triangles and other polygons. Compute the areas and perimeters in square cm and cm, if 1 geo square is 1 cm^2.

    Use a scale of 1 cm is 1 m. Now what are the areas and perimeters?

    Change the scale to 1 geo square is 5 km^5. Compute the areas and perimeters.

    Use other scales.

2. Change the whole. Form a rectangle of 3 by 4 on the geoboard. If 1 geosquare is 1 km^2, what is the measure of the rectangle   If the rectangle has a measurement of 1 square km, now what is the measure of one small square in the rectangle?
    Use other figures and change your whole.

3. Find as many shapes as possible with areas of 12 cm^2, 10 cm^2, 15 cm^2, . . ., if one geo square is 1 cm^2.

4. If from one nail across to the next nail is 1 dm, find as many shapes as possible that have perimeters of 24 dm, 18 dm, 15 dm, 7 dm, . . .

5. Form the square numbers letting one geo line unit be 1 km.
    Compare the areas and perimeters.

    Compare the number of nailheads in the interior not touching the bands.

    Compare the number of nails touched by the bands in forming each square number.

6. Let ⊢────┤ be 1 cm. Using the bands from nail to nail, what is the longest trail you can travel that doesn't retrace nor intersect itself?

7. Let ⊢────┤ be 1 dm. What is the perimeter of the largest rectangle you can form on the metric geoboard? (Be certain you know the definition of a rectangle) What is the perimeter of the smallest rectangle?

8. Form designs on the board with the bands.

9. Using the actual dimensions of the geo square — 2.5 cm x 2.5 cm, figure the area of the geo square. Form other squares and rectangles and compute their areas and perimeters.

10. Let the geo unit square be 1 mm^2. Can you form triangles with areas of 1 mm^2, 2 mm^2, 3 mm^2, 4 mm^2, 5 mm^2, 6 mm^2, 50 mm^2, 36 mm^2, 60 mm^2, 23 mm^2, others?

ON THE CM GRID

Follow the direction arrows as many centimeters as you are told by drawing connected line segments.

Start at ●

Connect the following segments:

1.	2 cm ←		Start again at *	
2.	3 cm ↑	12.	1 cm ↓	
3.	3 cm →	13.	6 cm ←	
4.	1 cm ↓	14.	2 cm ↑	
5.	1 cm ←	15.	6 cm →	
6.	4 cm ↓	16.	1 cm ↓	
7.	3 cm →	17.	2 cm →	
8.	4 cm ↑	18.	4 cm ↑	
9.	2 cm ←	19.	3 cm ←	
10.	2 cm ↓	20.	4 cm ↓	
11.	1 cm ← STOP.	21.	1 cm →	

What is the perimeter of the entire figure?
_____

What is the area of figure:

a. _____

b. _____

c. _____

d. _____

What is the total area of just the 3 intersections (∩)?
_____

What is the total area covered by the entire figure (∪)?
_____

What is the area of the exterior?
_____

ON THE CM GRID

Follow the direction arrows as many centimeters as you are told by drawing a broken line on the cm grid.

Start at •
draw the following segments:

1. 4 cm →
2. 1 cm ↑
3. 4 cm ←
4. 1 cm ↑
5. 3 cm →
6. 1 cm ↑
7. 3 cm ←
8. 1 cm ↑
9. 2 cm →
10. 1 cm ↑
11. 2 cm ←
12. 1 cm ↑
13. 1 cm →
14. 1 cm ↑
15. 1 cm ←
16. 1 cm ↑
17. 1 cm ←
18. 1 cm ↓
19. 1 cm ←
20. 1 cm ↓

21. 1 cm →
22. 1 cm ↓
23. 2 cm ←
24. 1 cm ↓
25. 2 cm →
26. 1 cm ↓
27. 3 cm ←
28. 1 cm ↓
29. 3 cm →
30. 1 cm ↓
32. 4 cm ←
32. 1 cm ↓
33. 4 cm →
34. 1 cm ↓
35. 2 cm ←
36. 1 cm ↓
37. 5 cm →
38. 1 cm ↑
39. 2 cm ←
40. 1 cm ↑

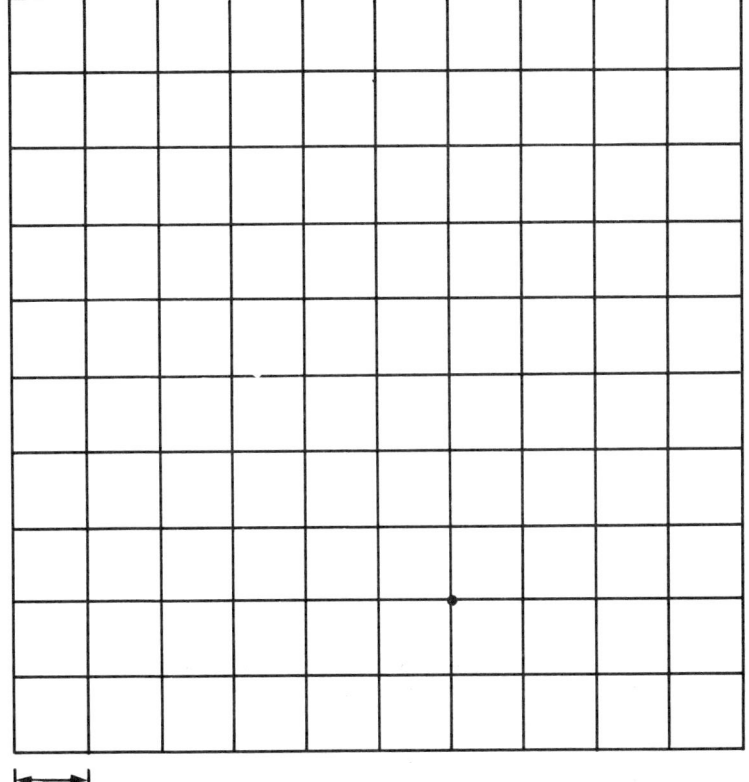

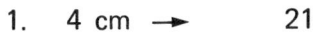
1 cm

1 cm²

What is the perimeter of the closed curve? _____

How many cm² in the region? _____

How many cm² in the exterior? _____

Color the region of the figure as follows:
    (All connecting)   3 cm² = Red
                              5 cm² = Brown
                              7 cm² = Orange
                              9 cm² = Purple
                              1 cm² = Yellow

METRIC TANGRAMS

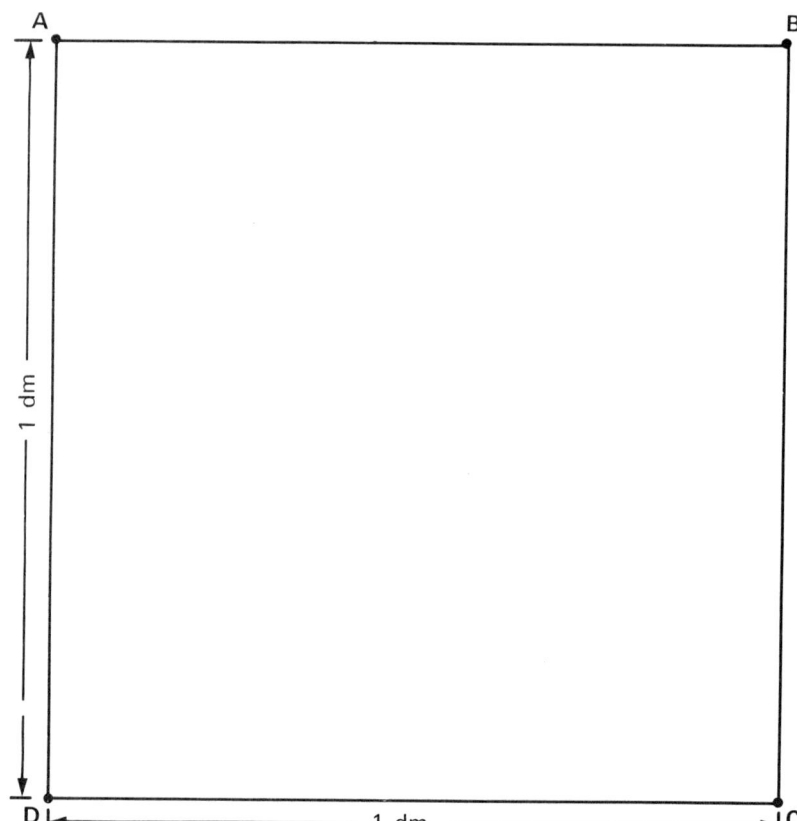

1. Connect B to D and measure to nearest cm.
   _____ cm

2. Place pt E 5 cm from pt B on $\overline{BC}$. $\overline{EC}$ is _____ cm

3. Place pt F 5 cm from pt C on $\overline{CD}$. $\overline{FD}$ is _____ cm

4. Draw $\overline{EF}$ and measure to nearest cm.
   _____ cm

5. Place pt G 35 mm from E along $\overline{EF}$.

6. Draw $\overline{AG}$ label the intersection with $\overline{BD}$ as pt H.
   $\overline{AG}$ is _____ cm.

7. Place pt I at the midpoint of $\overline{BH}$.
   $\overline{BH}$ is _____ cm.
   $\overline{IB}$ is _____ cm

8. Connect $\overline{IE}$ and measure
   $\overline{IE}$ is _____ cm

9. Place pt J 3.5 cm from pt D along $\overline{DH}$.

10. Connect and measure
    $\overline{JG}$ _____ cm

11. Find the area of:

    △ AHD = _____ cm²
    △ JHG = _____ cm²
    △ BHA = _____ cm²
    △ BIE = _____ cm²
    △ ECF = _____ cm²
    ▱ DFGJ = _____ cm²
    ▢ HIEG = _____ cm²

Total 100 cm² = 1 dm²

Cut out the seven pieces to form a set of tangrams, use all 7 pieces to:
   Reform the square.
   Form one large triangle.
   Form a rectangle.

Find other shapes you can make from the 7 tangrams.

52

Metric System of Measurement © Activity Resources Co. Hayward, CA 94540

A and P OF RECTANGLES IN METRIC
(Including squares)

```
      5 km
  M ─────────── N
  │             │
3 km  AREA = 15 km²
  │  PERIMETER = 16 km
  │             │
  P ─────────── O
```

If the sides of a ▭ are 5 km and 3 km, then the area is ____ km² and the perimeter is ____ km.

If the area of a ▭ is 15 km² and the perimeter is 16 km, what are the measurements of the two sides? _____ km and _____ km

Find the missing parts of rectangles:

	SIDE	SIDE	AREA	PERIMETER
a	8 m	4 m		
b	9 cm		81 cm²	
c		10 km		42 km
d			72 m²	34 m
e			42 km²	34 km
f	25 cm		225 cm²	
g			143 mm²	48 mm
h		11 dm		58 dm
*i	6 cm	20 mm		
j			68 m²	42 m

*Be Careful!

AREA cm², mm²

Find the areas of the stamps using mm² and cm² (Measure to nearest .5 cm)

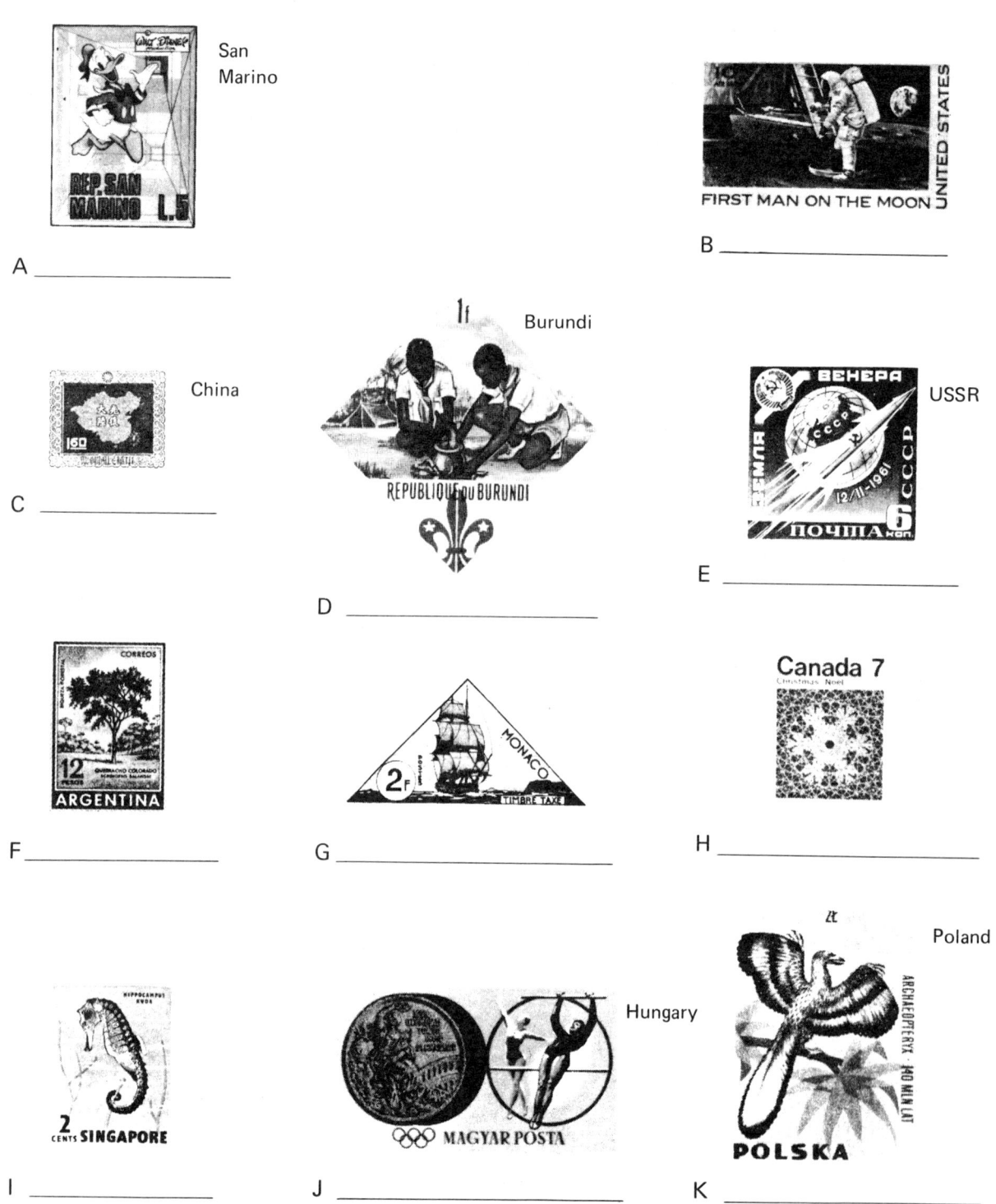

A _____

B _____

C _____

D _____

E _____

F _____

G _____

H _____

I _____

J _____

K _____

Can you find the places on a world map?

AREA M²

Find the Area in m² of these rooms of this floor plan (Take line measurements to the nearest ½m)

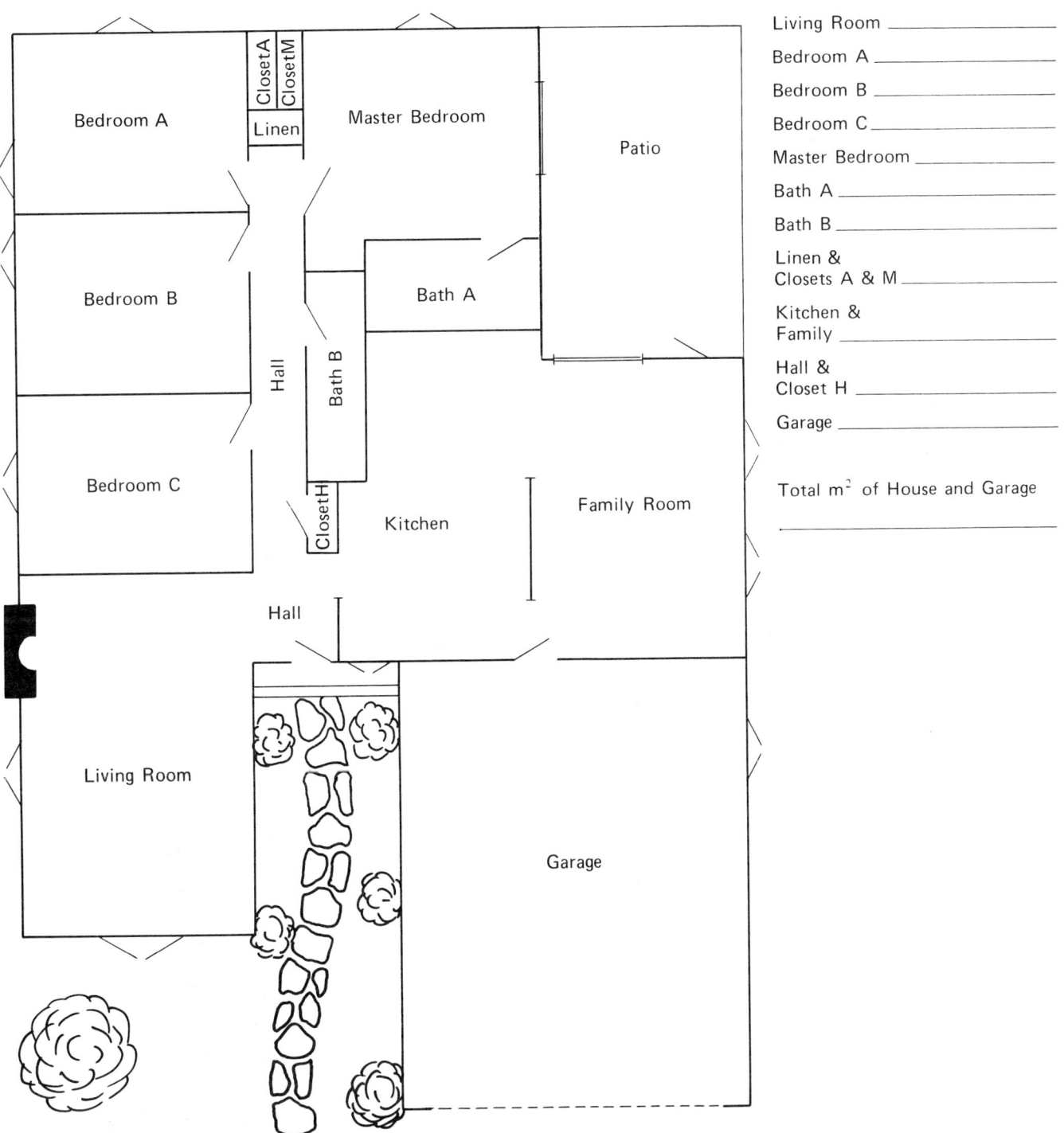

Living Room _____
Bedroom A _____
Bedroom B _____
Bedroom C _____
Master Bedroom _____
Bath A _____
Bath B _____
Linen & Closets A & M _____
Kitchen & Family _____
Hall & Closet H _____
Garage _____

Total m² of House and Garage
_____

Design a plan for a house with a smaller m², a larger m².

SCALE:
|—————|—————|
|————— 4m —————|

NOMOGRAPH

Metric x and ÷

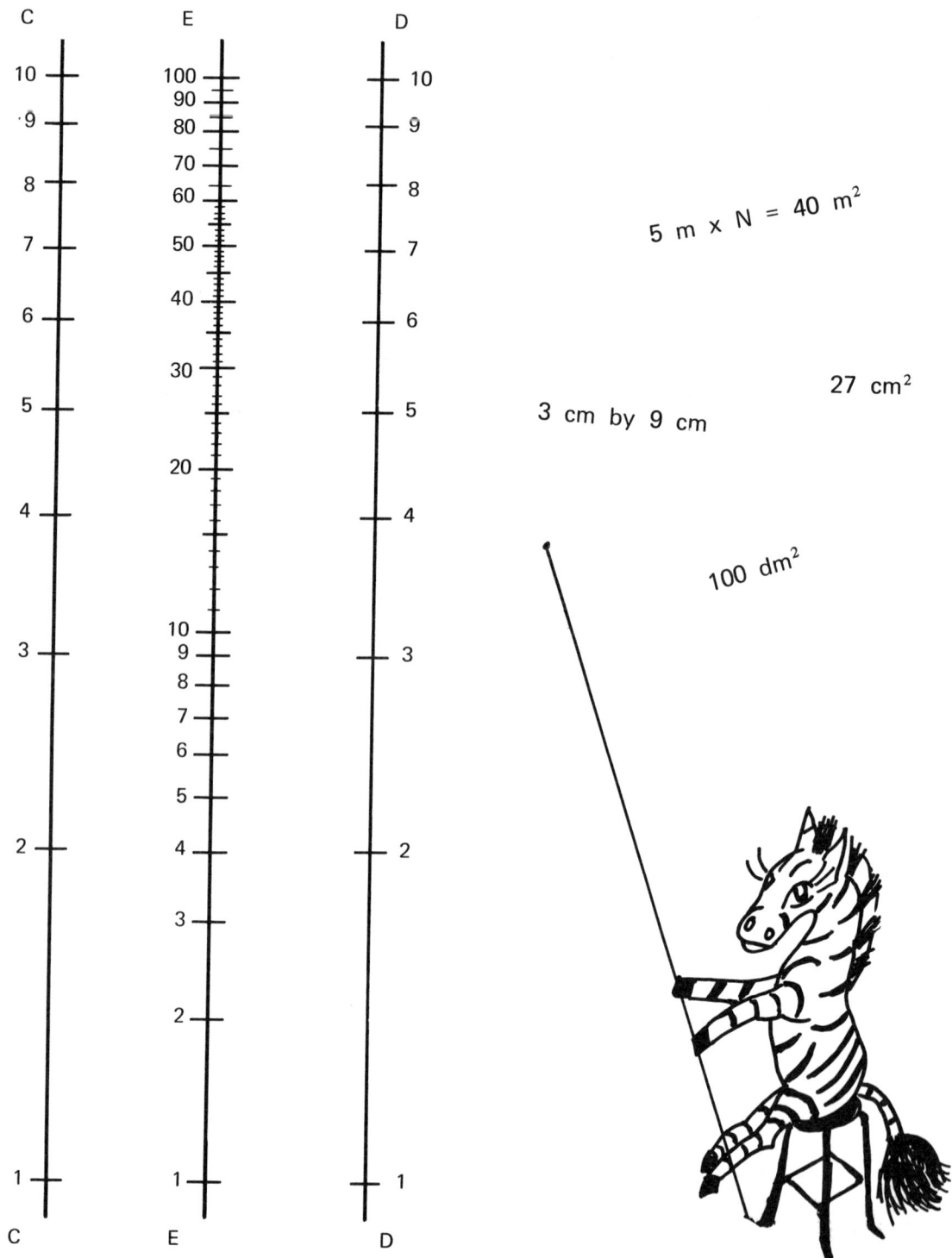

$5 \text{ m} \times N = 40 \text{ m}^2$

27 cm^2

3 cm by 9 cm

100 dm^2

Base 10: a nomograph for x and ÷

NOMOGRAPH

Metric x and ÷

Use a straight edge (Ruler, bottom of this page, thin stick like a skewer or swab stick.)

 Join a factor from line C with a factor on line D.
Read product on line E.

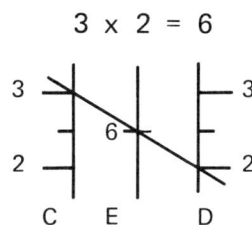

Does it work if you place 2 on C and 3 on D?

Join product on E with factor on C and read missing factor on D.

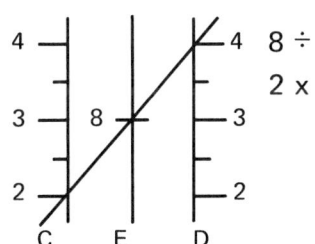

$8 \div 2 = N$
$2 \times N = 8$
$N = 4$

cm cm Area	A cm cm
3 by 3 = _____	35 cm² = 7 by _____
2 by 6 = _____	56 cm² = 8 by _____
7 by 7 = _____	48 cm² = 6 by _____
9 by 6 = _____	40 cm² = 8 by _____
1 by 5 = _____	100 cm² = 10 by _____
3 by 8 = _____	63 cm² = 7 by _____
4 by 9 = _____	15 cm² = 3 by _____
10 by 6 = _____	72 cm² = 9 by _____
8 by 8 = _____	32 cm² = 4 by _____
7 by 3 = _____	20 cm² = 2 by _____

Could the problems be worked as
dm — dm²
m — m²
mm — mm²
km — km²
as well as the
cm — cm²?

IDEAS IN AREA MEASUREMENT
with materials probably found in your classroom or home

1. Use a meter stick or meter tape to find the dimensions of the floor of a room. Compute the area. Find the price of rugs in the newspaper ads. (They will probably be given in cost per sq. yd. Since a m^2 is only about .01 more than the sq. yd., the cost for the m^2 is only a few cents more and can be computed and added on.) What is the cost to put rugs of different qualities on the floor. Graph the results.

2. How many m^2 of glass are used in your classroom?

3. Find the areas of several flat surfaces in your classroom — your book covers, your desk, teachers desk, the flag, all the blackboard surface, all the bulletin board surface.

4. List five or more items around you whose surface would best be measured in:

mm^2	cm^2	dm^2	m^2
top of pencil	math paper	wall map	floor
_____	_____	_____	_____
_____	_____	_____	_____
_____	_____	_____	_____
_____	_____	_____	_____

5. Find the area of the license place on a car. How much glass is used in the car? What is the area of the circle that would enclose the tire? the steering wheel?

6. Look for colorful ads in papers and magazines. Measure the amount of the page in cm^2 that is used for the ad.

    Cut out the ads using geometric shapes and paste your shapes into an attractive collage.

7. Collect trade names from cartons or wrappers found about your house. (Kleenex, Campbells, Coca Cola, TV Dinner, Cheerios, etc.) Place each label on grid paper. Determine the rectangle that would enclose the name. Figure out the area.

8. Work out a square, a rectangle and a triangle that would form the sides of a region that measures 1 km^2. With stakes and string, and a meter tape measure, plot them on your school yard. How do you think an acre would compare with your 1 km^2?

9. Write a story or poem about the poor little cm^2 who just can't fit in with the other geometric figures.

Metric Volume Measurement

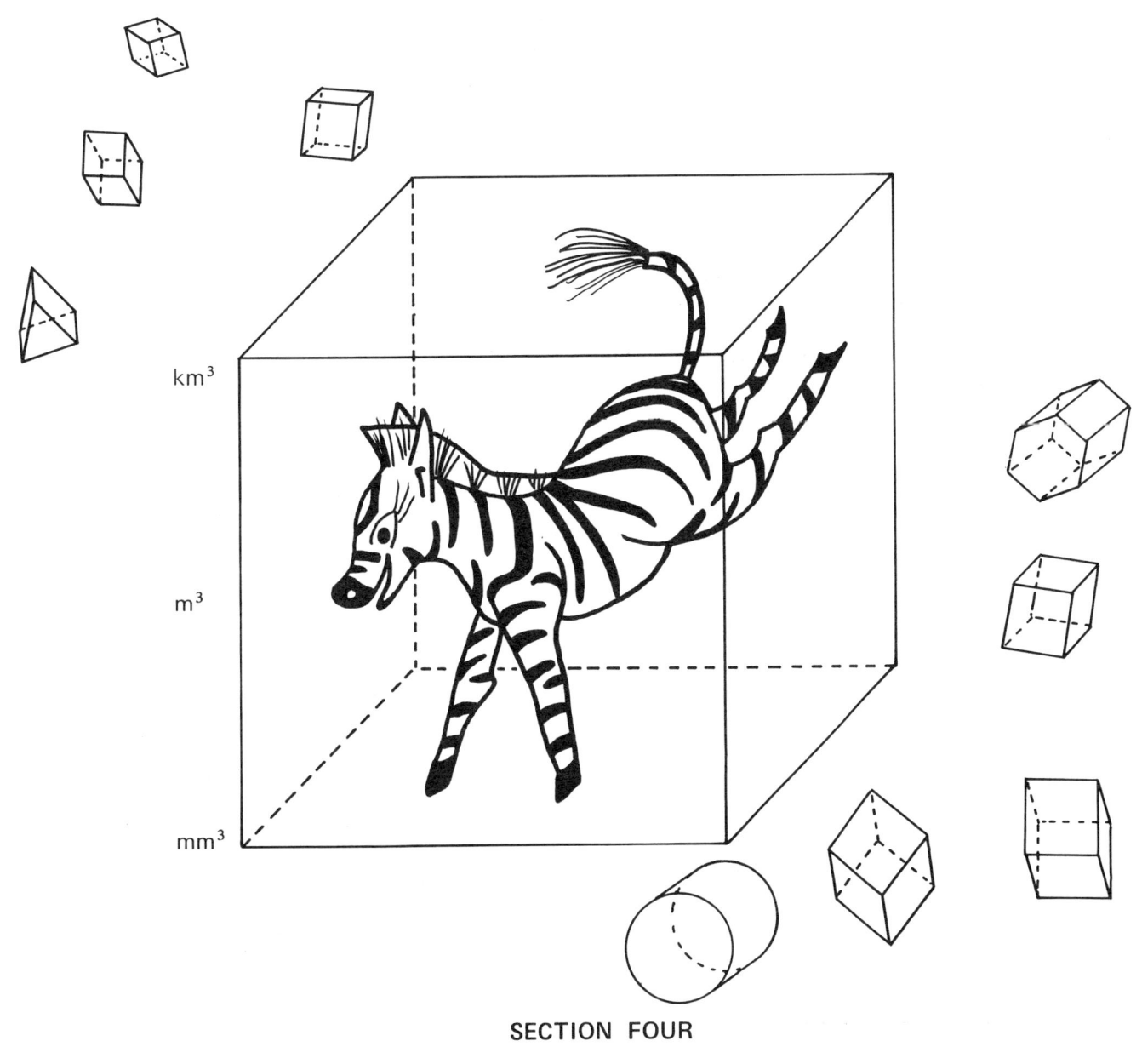

SECTION FOUR

SPACE MEASURE
Volume of Rectangular Prisms

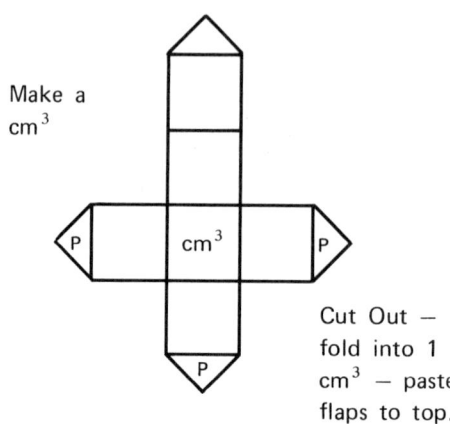

Make a cm³

Cut Out — fold into 1 cm³ — paste flaps to top.

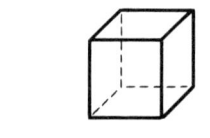

1 cm by 1 cm by 1 cm = 1 cm³

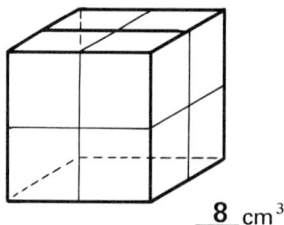

__8__ cm³

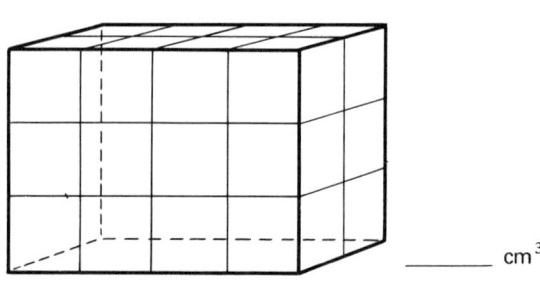

_____ cm³

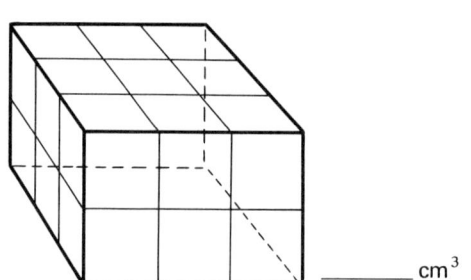

_____ cm³

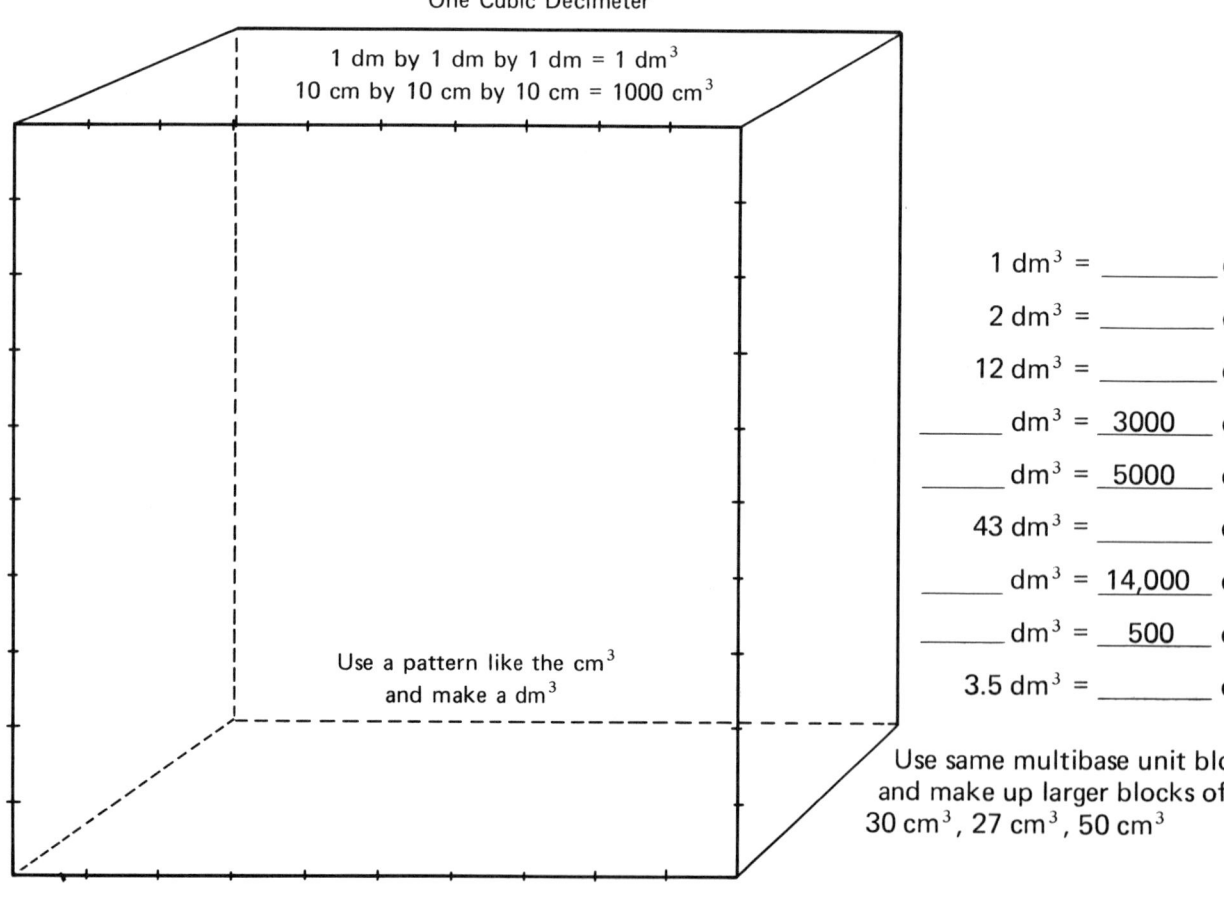

1 dm³ or 1 cu dm
One Cubic Decimeter

1 dm by 1 dm by 1 dm = 1 dm³
10 cm by 10 cm by 10 cm = 1000 cm³

Use a pattern like the cm³ and make a dm³

1 dm³ = _____ cm³

2 dm³ = _____ cm³

12 dm³ = _____ cm³

_____ dm³ = __3000__ cm³

_____ dm³ = __5000__ cm³

43 dm³ = _____ cm³

_____ dm³ = __14,000__ cm³

_____ dm³ = __500__ cm³

3.5 dm³ = _____ cm³

Use same multibase unit blocks and make up larger blocks of 30 cm³, 27 cm³, 50 cm³

VOLUME OF THESE RECTANGULAR PRISMS
3D

Volume = length x width x height

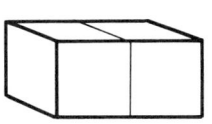

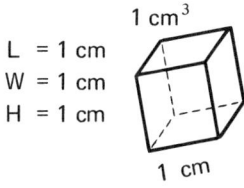

(a) $\underline{} 1 \times 1 \times 2 = \underline{}$
V = _____ cm³

$1 \times 1 \times 1 = 1^3 = 1$
V = 1 cm³

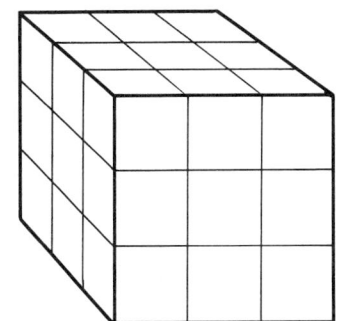

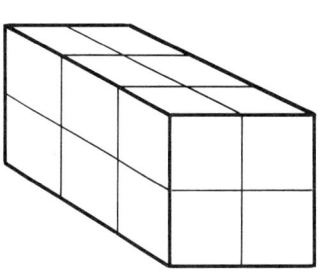

(b) _____ x _____ x _____ = _____
V = _____

(c) _____ x _____ x _____ = _____
V = _____

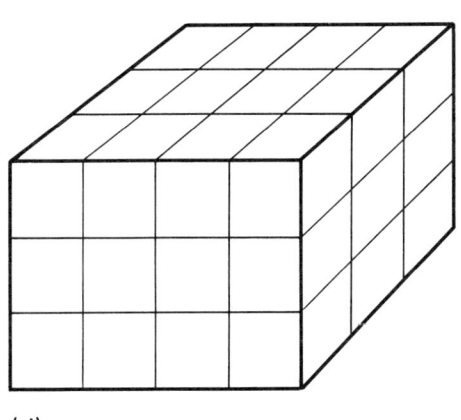

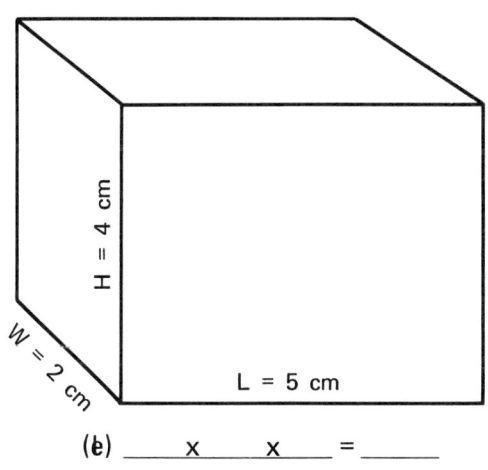

(d) _____ x _____ x _____ = _____
V = _____

(e) _____ x _____ x _____ = _____
V = _____

(f)

h	l	w	Volume
12 cm	4 cm	3 cm	cm³
8 cm	6 cm	10 cm	
25 m	3 m	7 m	
11 km	4 km	11 km	
1 dm	1 dm	1 dm	
7 dm	4 dm	6 dm	

PACKAGING

How many *different* sizes of cartons can you build that will hold 36 dm³ of cereal? All boxes must measure at least **2** on any side. Use only whole numbers.

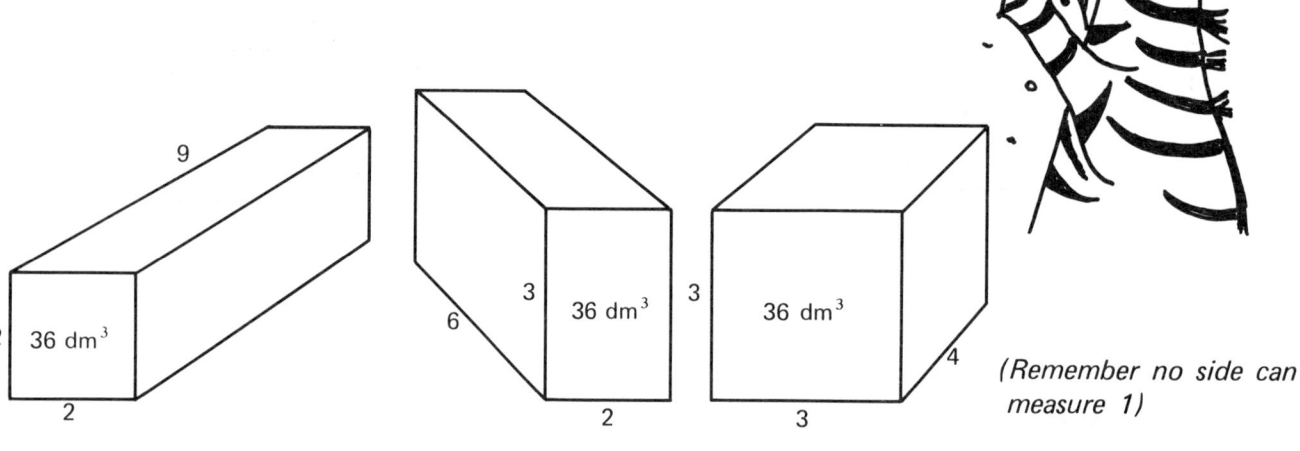

(Remember no side can measure 1)

VOLUME	HOW MANY	POSSIBLE CARTON SIZES	
36 dm³	3	2 dm x 2 dm x 9 dm 2 dm x 3 dm x 6 dm	3 dm x 3 dm x 4 dm
24 m³			
60 km³			
72 mm³			
100 km³			
84 cm³			

BUILD A CUBE

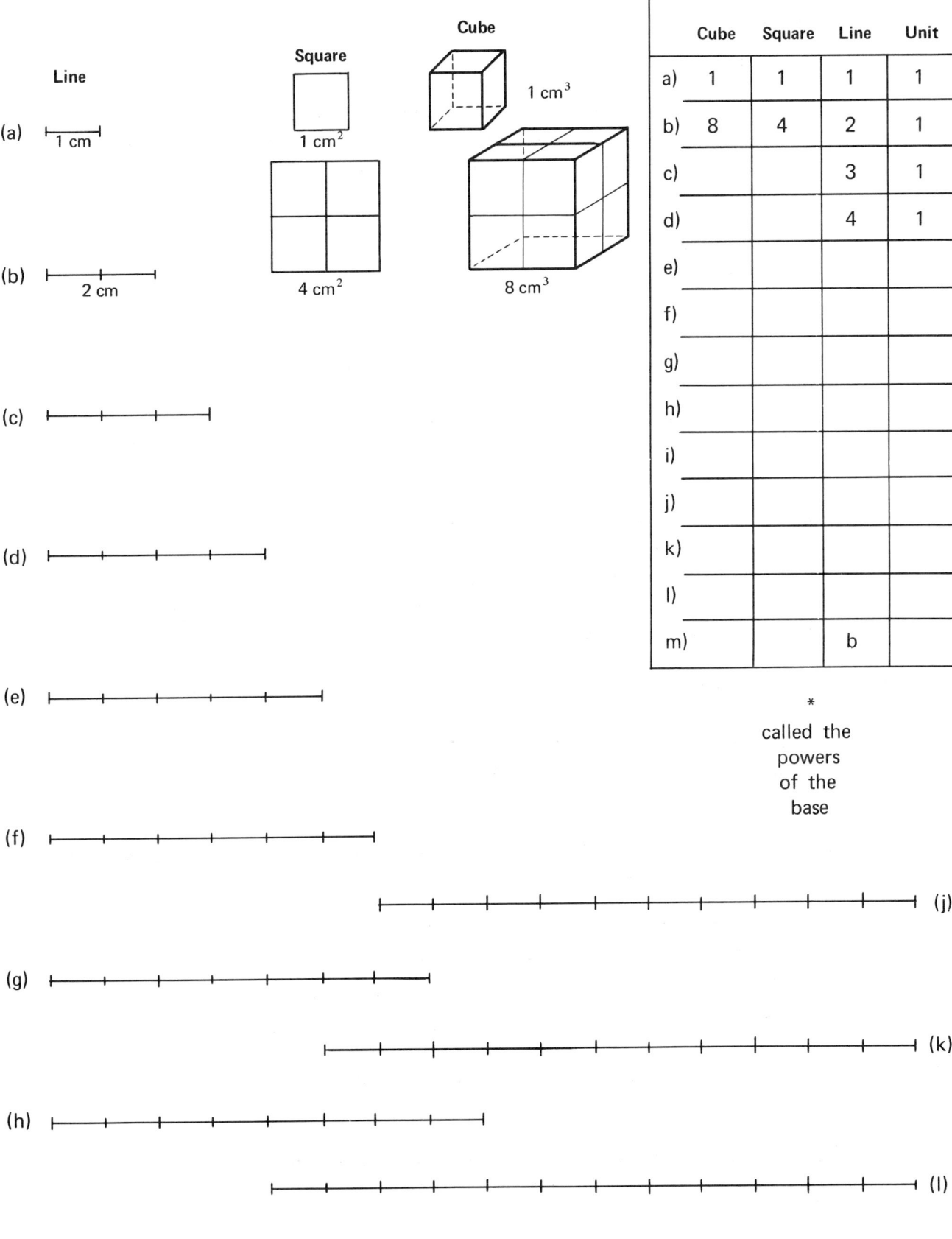

IDEAS IN VOLUME MEASUREMENT
with materials probably found in your classroom or home

1. What is the volume of a ream of paper? (500 sheets) How many reams would fill a paper carton that has the measurements 1 m x 1 m x 2 m? If every student in a school district of 50,000 students wastes one piece of paper a day, what is the volume of the wasted paper?

2. What is the volume of one sugar cube? How many cubes would fit into a box that measures 1 dm^3?

3. Measure with cm the length, width, and height of boxes found around the home. Work out volumes. Cereal boxes, soap boxes, games boxes, cracker boxes.

4. Use centimeter cubes from a set of multibase blocks. a) Build towers of various sizes and figure the space occupied. b) Build a 2^3, 3^3, 4^3, 5^3. c) Use the 10 cm rods and form 1 dm^3.

5. From this pattern drawn to the correct size on a piece of tag board form 1 dm^3. Use the dm^3 to find objects that would be about 1 dm^3 in size. Compare this dm^3 with the cm made from the pattern on page 54.

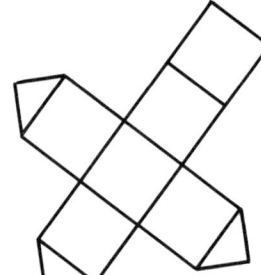

6. Could you make a m^3?

7. Name as many products as you can that are packaged for sale in markets using volume measure.

8. You are asked to crate the following items separately. Using metric measures, what would be the size of each crate.

    a piano _____
    refrigerator _____
    a TV set _____
    a bike _____

9. If everything were moved out of your classroom, how much air can fill the room? (What is the volume?)

10. Practice drawing rectangular prisms, triangular prisms and other 3-d figures by studying examples of this as is done in your math books.

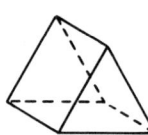 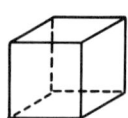 

Metric Liquid Capacity Measurement

SECTION FIVE

THE LITER (l)

What is a liter?

Take one decimeter   1 dm = 10 cm
Form a square $1 \text{ dm}^2 = 100 \text{ cm}^2$
Form a cube $1 \text{ dm}^3 = 1000 \text{ cm}^3$

the amount of liquid, as water, that fills this 1 dm^3 is One Liter, l.

Filled with water it's a LITER and weighs one kilogram!

Separate the dm^3 into 1000 cm^3

Fill 1 cm^3 with water — 1 ml.

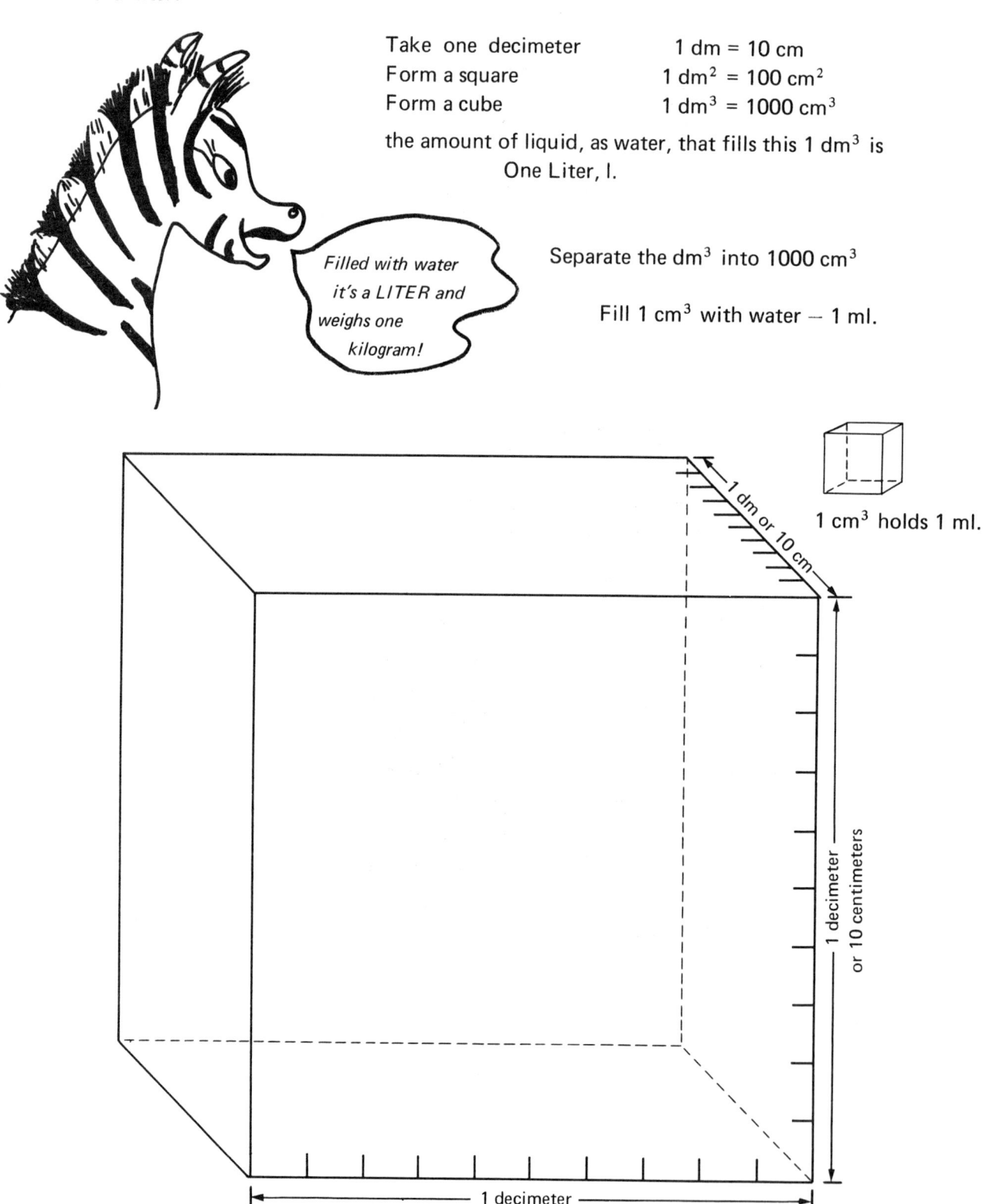

1 cm^3 holds 1 ml.

1 dm or 10 cm

1 decimeter or 10 centimeters

1 decimeter or 10 centimeters

LITER — LIQUID CAPACITY

1000 ml = 1 l   1000 l = 1 kl
100 cl = 1 l   100 l = 1 hl
10 dl = 1 l   10 l = 1 dal

(a) Relate Volume and liquid capacity

___1___ cm³ holds ___1___ ml
_____ cm³ holds ___1___ l
_____ cm³ holds ___3___ l
__500__ cm³ holds _____ l
__238__ cm³ holds _____ l
_____ cm³ holds _1.754_ l
___4___ cm³ holds _____ ml
_____ cm³ holds __29__ ml
___2___ dm³ holds _____ l
___2___ dm³ holds _____ ml
_____ dm³ holds _1500_ ml
_____ dm³ = 1500 cm³

(b) Build a container and find its liquid capacity.

Rectangular Prism Size	Volume	Liquid Capacity
3 by 5 by 7 cm	_____ cm³	_____ l
4 by 1 by 9 cm	_____	_____ l
8 by 10 by 6 dm	_____	_____ l
5 by 12 by 12 dm	_____	_____ l
6 by 4 by 8 m	_____ dm³	_____ l
2 by 10 by 9 m	_____ m³	_____ kl

(c) What sizes could the aquarium, a rectangular prism, be to hold the given amount of water?

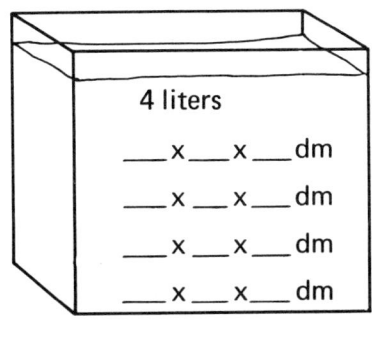

4 liters
___ x ___ x ___ dm
___ x ___ x ___ dm
___ x ___ x ___ dm
___ x ___ x ___ dm

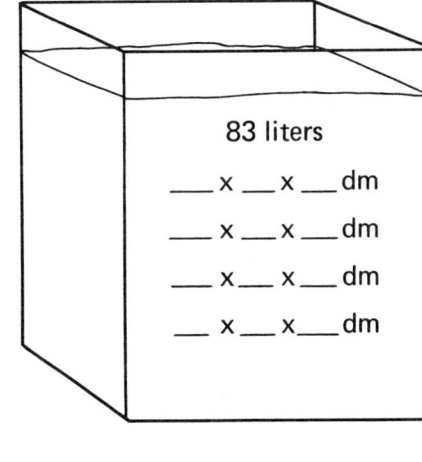

83 liters
___ x ___ x ___ dm
___ x ___ x ___ dm
___ x ___ x ___ dm
___ x ___ x ___ dm
___ x ___ x ___ dm

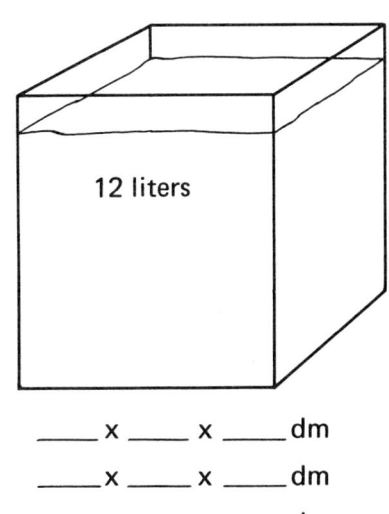

12 liters

___ x ___ x ___ dm
___ x ___ x ___ dm
___ x ___ x ___ dm
___ x ___ x ___ dm

TO MEASURE A LITER

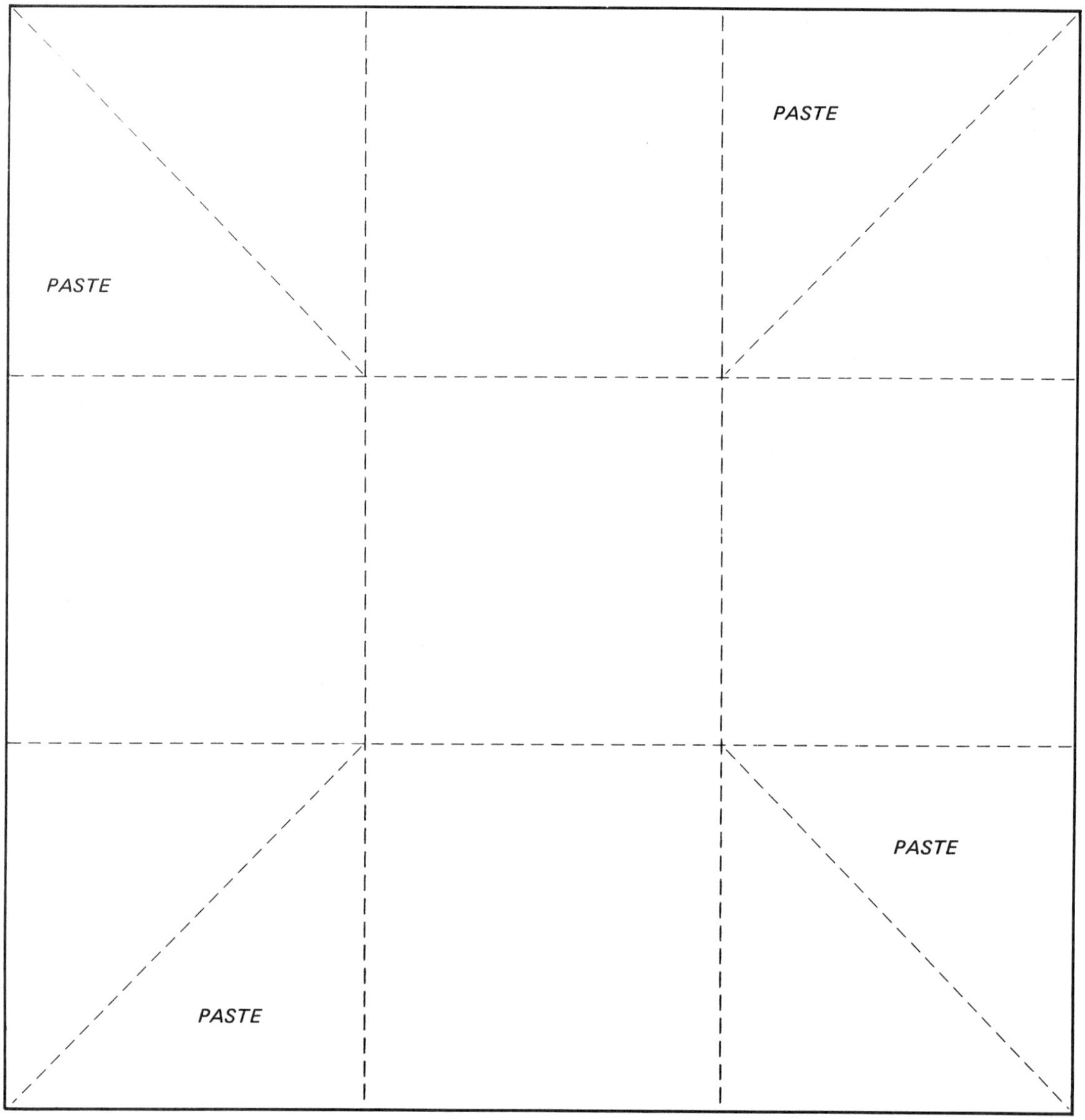

PASTE

PASTE

PASTE

PASTE

When this square is cut out and folded into a box, it measures 5 x 5 x 5 or 125 cm^3 or .125 dm^3 and holds 125 ml or .125 l. To measure one liter fill the measure 8 times.

If a 1 liter measure is preferred, draw a similar pattern increased to 30 cm x 30 cm x 30 cm.

Cut out the square and paste on tagboard or a good waterproof paper. Score and then fold on the dotted lines. Paste the tabs down on the outside of the box. Let dry thoroughly before using water in it. If waterproofing is needed, use a plastic sandwich bag as a lining.

TO MEASURE A LITER

Use your 125 ml measure and water.

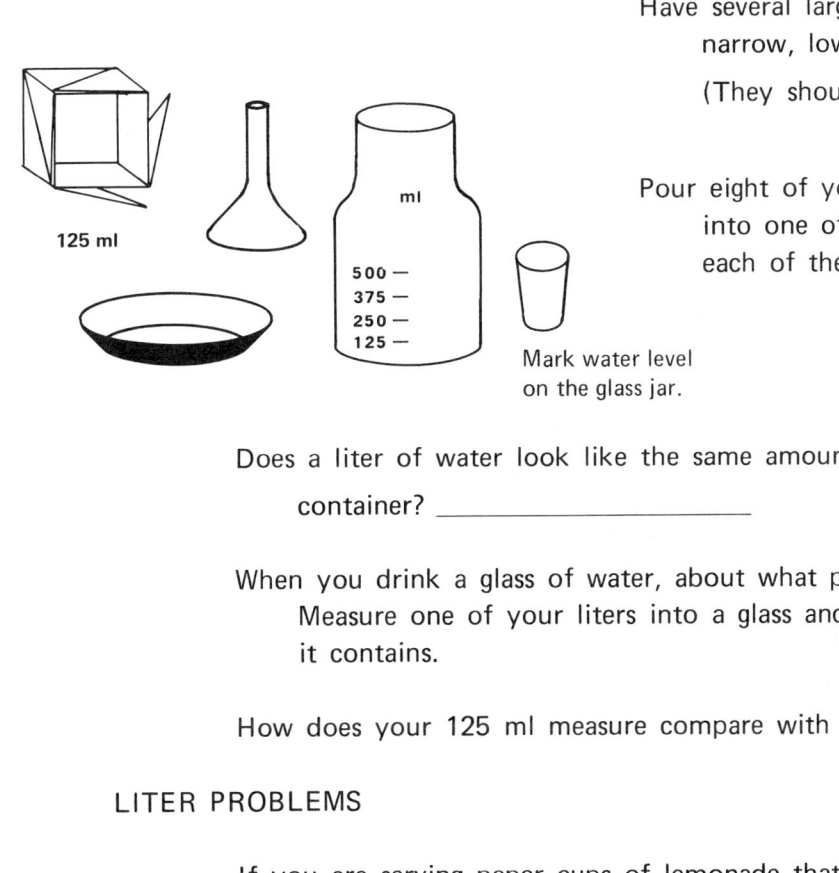

Have several large jars and pans . . . tall and narrow, low and flat, short and wide
(They should hold more than a quart.)

Pour eight of your 125 ml measures of water into one of the jars. Pour eight more into each of the others.

Mark water level on the glass jar.

Does a liter of water look like the same amount in each container? _____

When you drink a glass of water, about what part of a liter are you drinking? Measure one of your liters into a glass and find out how many glasses it contains.

How does your 125 ml measure compare with a glass? _____

LITER PROBLEMS

If you are serving paper cups of lemonade that measure 250 ml each, how many people could have drinks from six liters? _____

A rain guage showed 38 ml of rain fell over a period of 20 hours. How much rain fell, on an average, in one hour? _____

You buy a liter can of paint. You use ¾ of it to paint some booths for the school carnival. How many ml are left in the can?

_____

A motorcycle was getting 25 km for every liter of gasoline. How far can you travel on 5 liters of gas? _____

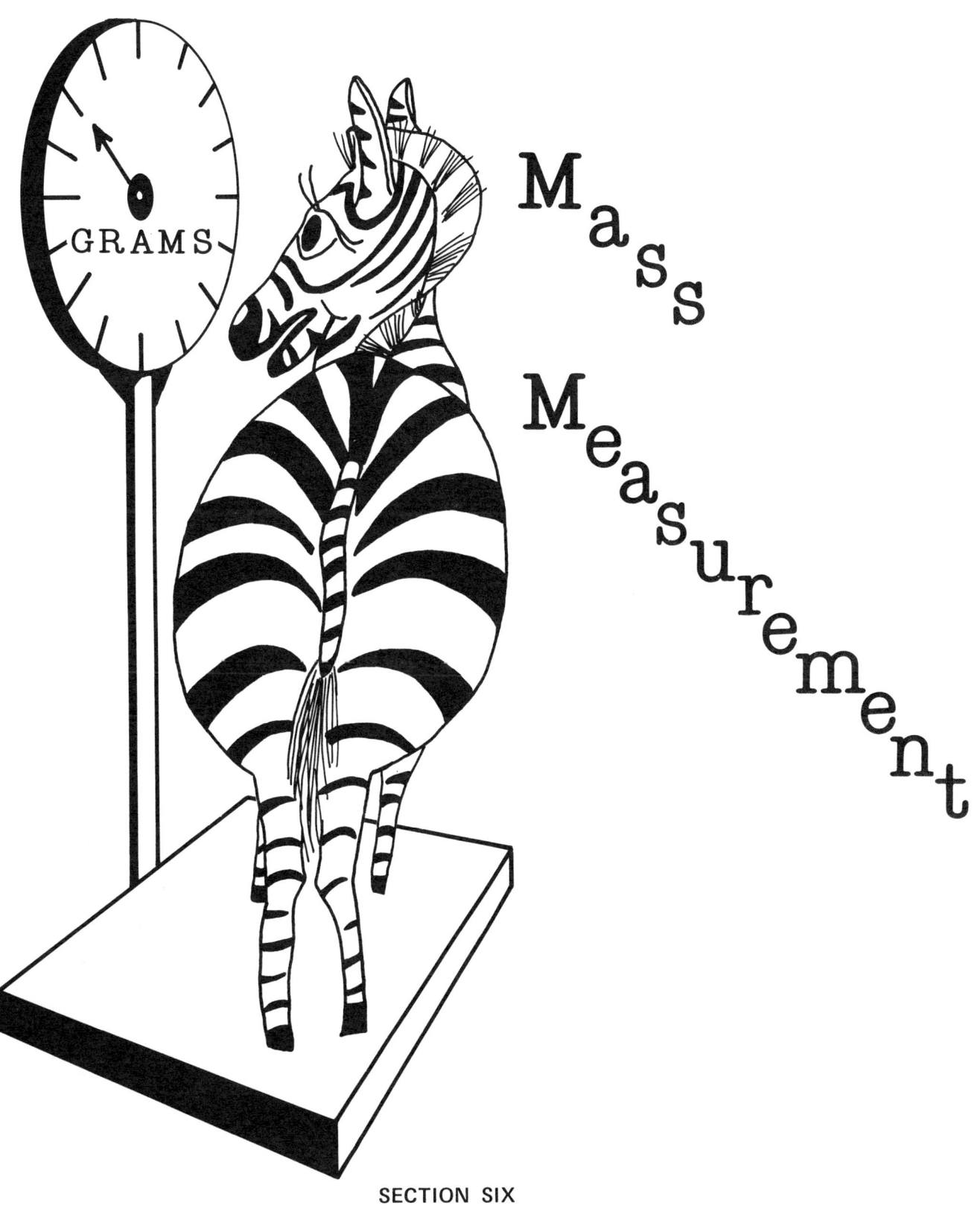

SECTION SIX

MASS — THE GRAM (g)

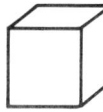

1 cm³ filled with water
mass is 1 g

1 dm³ = 1000 cm³ filled
with water has a mass of
1000 g = 1 kg

Separate 1 g into:
1000 parts —
1 mg
100 parts
1 cg
10 parts
1 dg

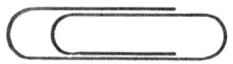

1 paper clip (medium size)
mass is about 1 g

1 nickel
about 5 g

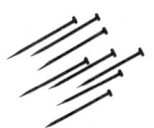

8 pins about 1 gm

What other things can you find with a mass of about —

1 g	5 g	10 g = 1 dkg	1000 g = 1 kg
___	___	___	___
___	___	___	___
___	___	___	___

380 g = _____ kg   10 g = _____ cg
2500 g = _____ kg   8.7 g = _____ cg
_____ g = 5.7 kg   _____ g = 2.46 cg
_____ g = .912 kg   _____ g = 22 cg
_____ mg = 4 g   _____ mg = 17 cg
_____ mg = 1.8 g   _____ mg = 157 cg
3500 mg = _____ g   246 mg = _____ cg
7652 mg = _____ g   53 mg = _____ cg

COMPARE THE GRAM TO OTHER METRIC UNITS

1 cm³ filled with water measures 1 ml and has a mass of 1 g.
1 dm³ filled with water measures 1 l and has a mass of 1 kg.

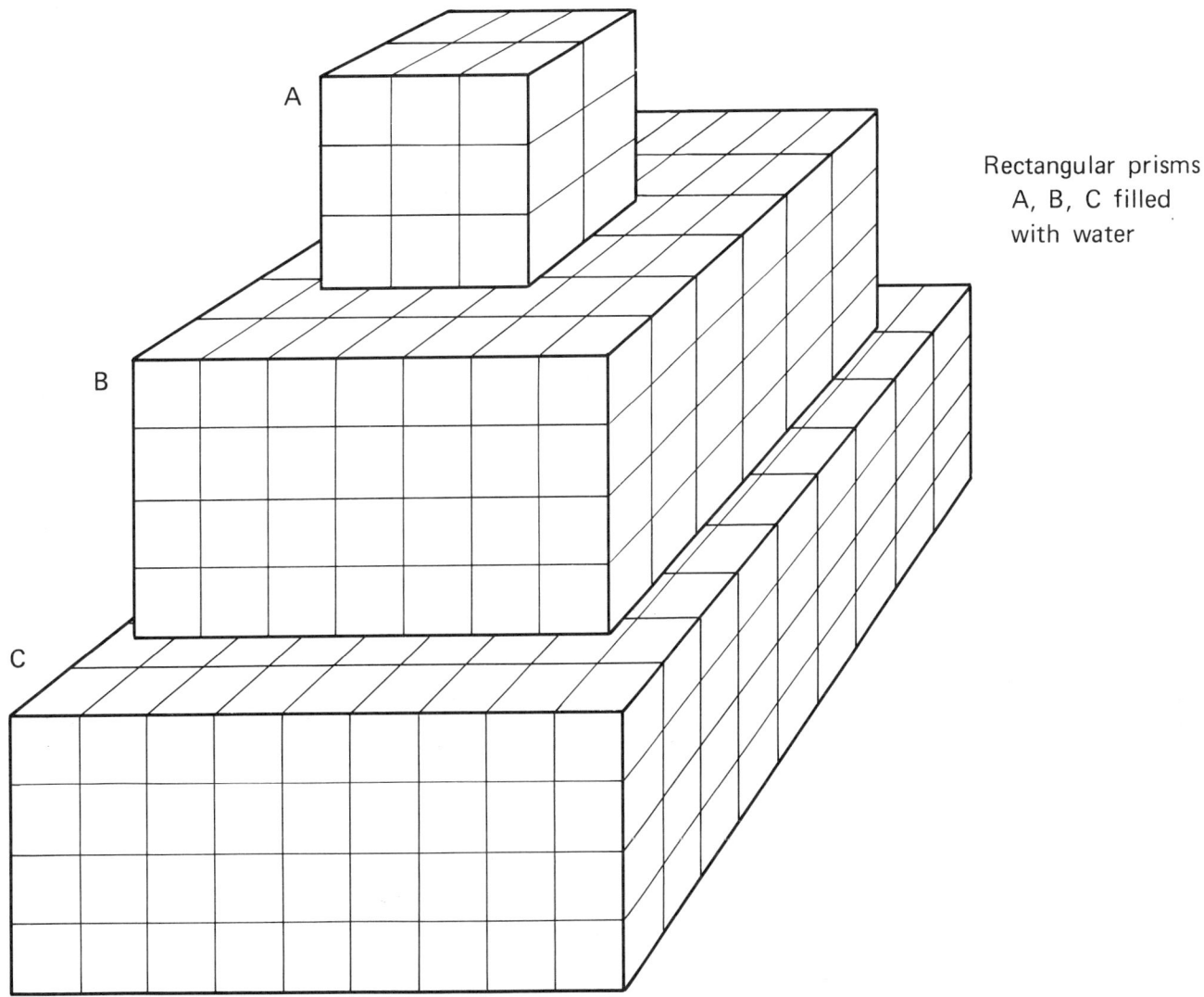

Rectangular prisms A, B, C filled with water

	VOLUME cm³	LIQUID CAPACITY in l	MASS IN g AND IN kg
A			
B			
C			
Entire Tower			

BALANCE Copy the patterns on a heavy cardboard...

FLAT TOP

Cut out pattern . . .

Score then fold on dotted lines.

Paste tabs A & B to back of side X; tabs C & D to back of side Y.

Put a small tight rubber band* around the center of flat top.

FULCRUM

Cut out pattern.

Score and fold on dotted lines.

Slide piece under rubber band.

Paste part R under part S to form triangular fulcrum.

Small cup cake liners can be pasted at each end of the flat top rather than using the fold-up sides if so desired.

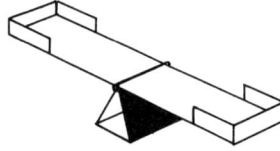

*If a long band is used and is lapped 2 or 3 times to tighten, see that the top is under just one lap of the band. This is a must for proper teetering.

MASS

Use a balance scale or make your own with cardboard as described on the last page.

Use the scale and gram pieces such as,
centicubes...
or
some small object, as a
paper clip.

a. Look around the classroom and outdoors for small objects to weigh on your scale. Record the object and its mass.

object	mass
_____	_____
_____	_____
_____	_____
_____	_____

b. What is the mass of: Compute the mass of:

   5 beans   _____ g   5,000 beans   _____
   10 rice grains _____ g   10,000 grains   _____
   5 gum wrappers _____ g   1,000 wrappers   _____
   8 toothpicks   _____ g   400 toothpicks   _____

c. Take a cm^3 wooden block, a cm^3 plastic block, a cm^3 paper block (pattern on p. 54), a cm^3 block made of clay. Weigh each cm^3. Do all cm^3 have the same mass?

   _____   _____
   _____   _____

d. Select a small ball of clay. Weigh it. _____
   Remove the clay but not the mass pieces on the scale.

   Reshape the clay into a worm. Use all of the clay. Weigh the worm. _____

   Reshape the worm into a tiny starfish. Use all of the clay. Weigh the starfish _____

   Reshape several times weighing your shape each time.

   _____   _____   _____

   What are your conclusions about mass and shape?

IDEAS IN LIQUID CAPACITY AND MASS MEASUREMENT
with materials probably round in your classroom or home

1. With scales or balances compare the masses of various objects in the room. Arrange them in the order of lightest to heaviest.

2. Weigh the unit block of a multibase set or the unit rod of a relationship set. Build towers of blocks or rods. Compute the mass of the towers.

3. If a scale that measures kilograms is available, weigh members of the class and graph the results. If no scale is available, weigh the students in pounds and convert to kg. (Page 75 in this book can help with this.)

4. Gather cans and bottles of various shapes and sizes. Use arbitrary units of measure and find the capacity of each. Use a standard liter and find the measurements.

5. Use a quart milk bottle and the standard liter and compare them by using water.

6. Build rectangular prisms out of blocks that are 1 cm^3 in volume. Compute the volume and determine the amount of water that would be needed to fill the prism if it were hollow. Also determine how much the water would weigh.

7. A kilogram cake? Take simple recipes from a cookbook. Rewrite the directions using metric. Actually cook one of your recipes.

8. Figure out convenient sized packages, cans, bottles, cartons, for materials bought in stores using metric measurement.

	Measurement	Package
Butter	2 kg 4 cubes, .5 kg each	about the size of 1 lb.
Milk		
Pop		
Potatoes		
Berries		
Soup		
Cereal		
Gasoline		

Metric : Customary
Customary : Metric
Comparison

SECTION SEVEN

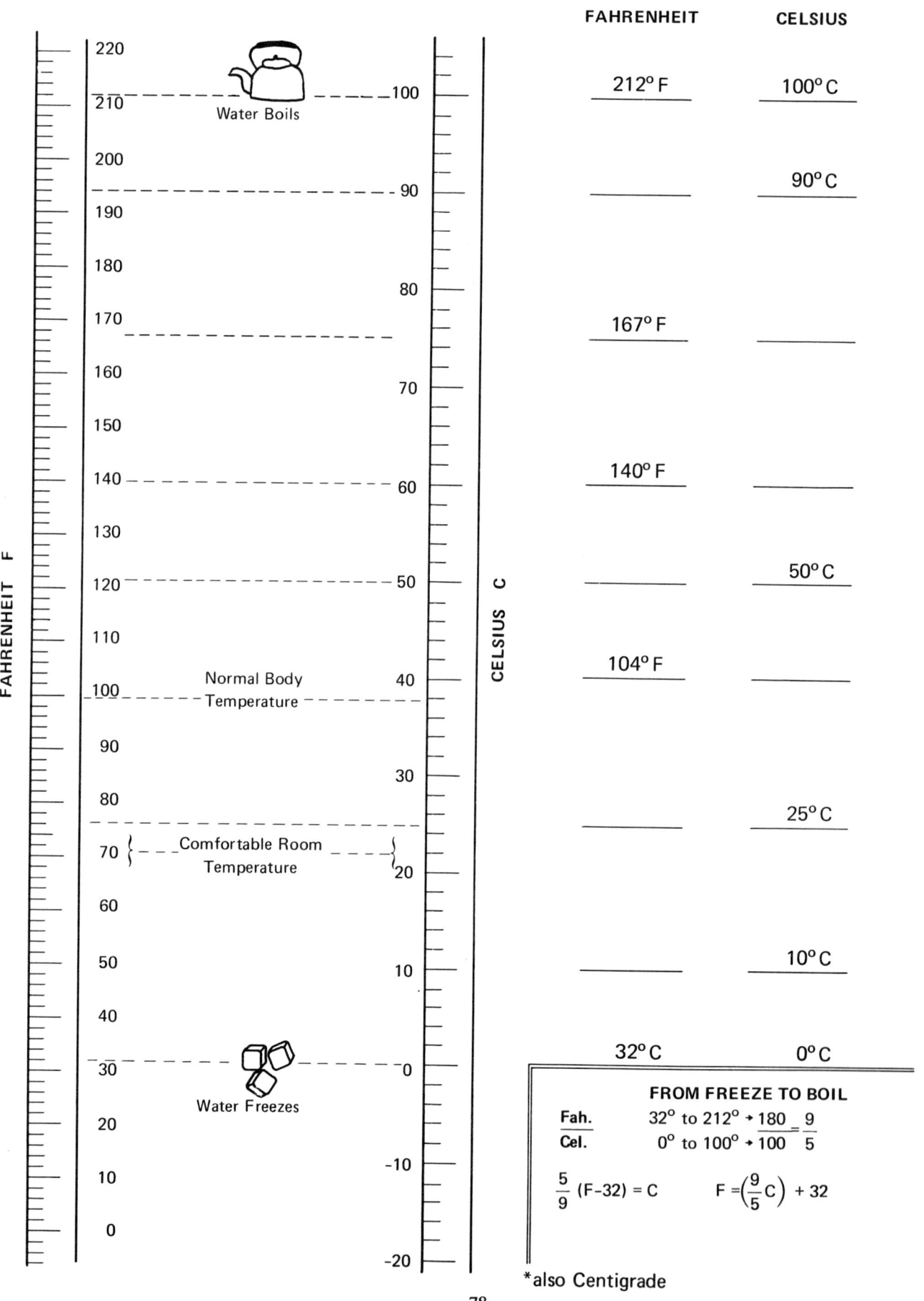

TEMPERATURE: Use the Fahrenheit F Scale and the Celsius C Scale.

1. Your popsicle is placed in a refrigerator at 32°C. Will it keep? _____

2. Your bath water measures 45°C. Will you shiver? _____

3. Your teakettle has just started to boil. Is it now just 212°C? _____

4. Ice has begun to form on a puddle, the thermometer reads 0°C. Right? _____

5. There is more heat needed to raise the Fahrenheit thermometer 10°F than the Centigrade thermometer 10°C. Right? _____

6. It's 50°C, do you need a fan? _____

7. There are 100° on Celsius from water freezing to water boiling. Right? _____

8. The Doctor uses a thermometer and says you have a 35°C temperature. Are you above normal? _____

9. C temperatures in the seventies are comfortable for a schoolroom. Right? _____

10. Temperature readings can go below zero on F scale but not on the C scale. Right? _____

CONVERTER OF LENGTH

Linear

mm cm   in
     0 —   — 0
  5
 10   1
      2
      3   — 1
      4
 50   5   — 2
      6
      7
      8   — 3
      9
100 10   — 4

Use your cm and inch rulers to continue the converter to 18 cm.

1 in. is about _____ cm

5 cm is about _____ in

3.5 in is about _____ cm

13 cm is about _____ in

Without using your ruler draw a line segment 6 in long and another 6 cm long. Measure. How close were you? Name each in the other system.

Practice drawing other lengths and checking with your ruler.

Guess the lengths of small items in your classroom in cm and in. Verify with your ruler.

Can you change cm — in and in — cm without using any help?

15 cm is about _____ in

8½ in is about _____ cm

20 in is about _____ cm

42 cm is about _____ in

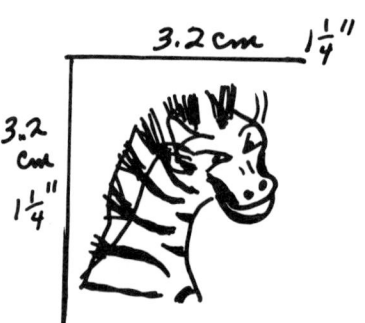

80

Metric System of Measurement © Activity Resources Co. Hayward, CA 94540

HOW MUCH DO YOU WEIGH? HOW TALL? CONVERTERS

Complete the chart and graph the results

		HEIGHT cm	MASS kg
Students	A	6'2"		220 lb	
	B	3'7"		66 lb	
	C	5'2"		121 lb	
	D	49"	125	95 lb	43
	E	68"		172 lb	
	F	4'7"		110 lb	
You	G				

Bar Graph of height in cm / mass in kg

MASS CONVERTER

COMPARISON

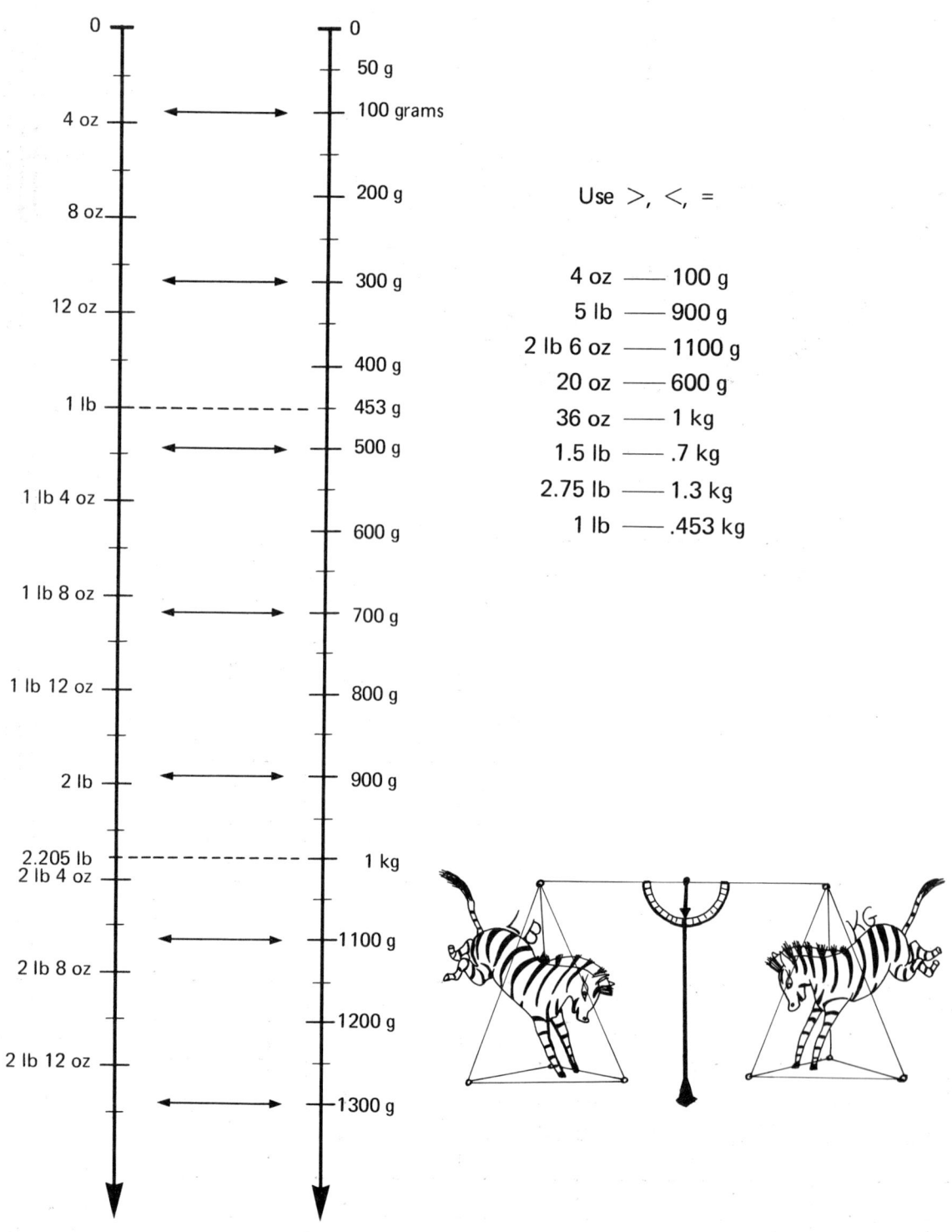

Use >, <, =

4 oz —— 100 g
5 lb —— 900 g
2 lb 6 oz —— 1100 g
20 oz —— 600 g
36 oz —— 1 kg
1.5 lb —— .7 kg
2.75 lb —— 1.3 kg
1 lb —— .453 kg

LIQUID CONVERTER

COMPARE

Use >, <, =

1 l —— 1 qt
.5 l —— 1 cup
2500 ml —— 88 oz
3000 ml —— 3 qt
1.5 l —— 3.5 pt
1000 ml —— 40 oz
.750 l —— 16 oz
1 l —— 1.057 qt

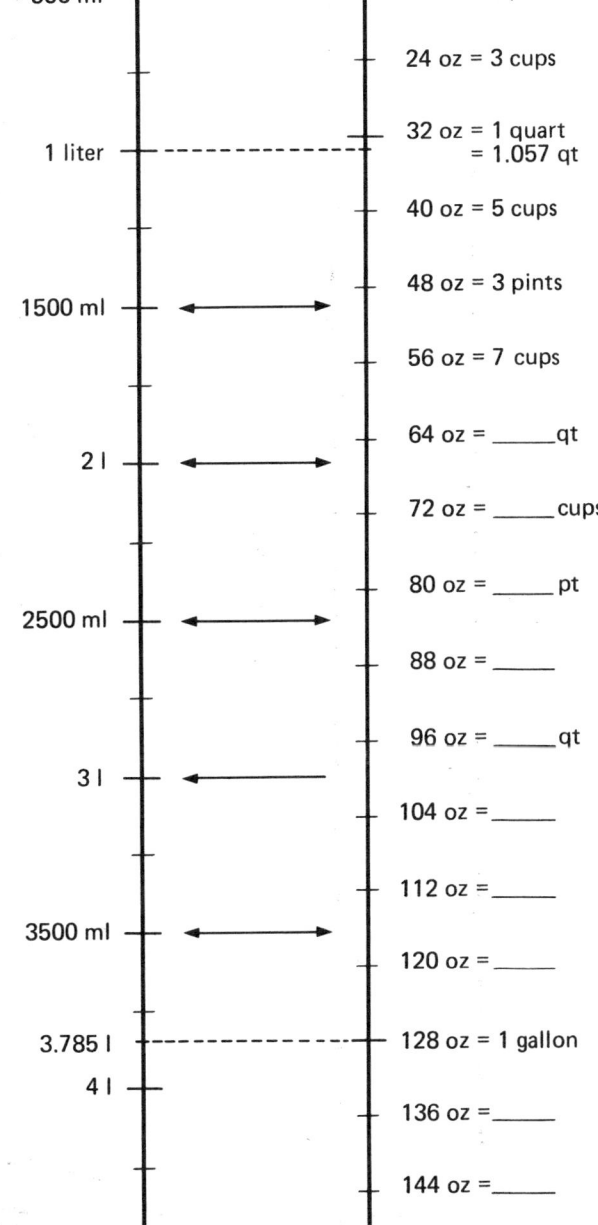

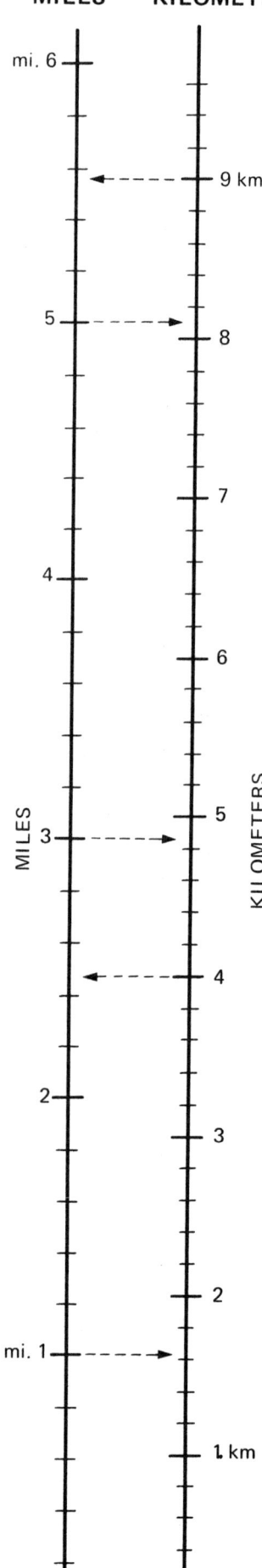

MILES   KILOMETERS   CONVERTER

Use this miles km converter and any of the other converters on pages 71-82 to help answer the questions.

You are an athlete at a track meet.

1. You run the mile, 4 laps, around the track. That measures _____ km

2. One lap measures _____ km

3. 8 laps is called the _____ mi run or _____ km

4. You run a cross country race of 24 mi. _____ km

5. You high jump 1.8 m or about _____ in

6. You long jump 21 feet. In metric that would be _____ m

7. You pick up the 5 pound shot put. It weighs _____ kg

8. You go over the pole vault at 17 feet or _____ m

9. The temperature reads 104° F. It's hot! Metric reads. _____ c

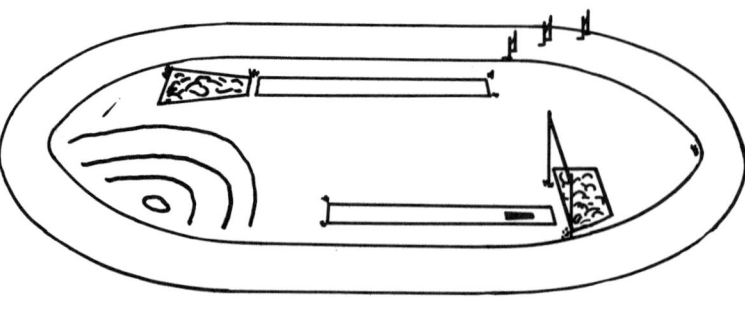

84

Metric System of Measurement © Activity Resources Co. Hayward, CA 94540

COMPUTING WHICH IS EASIER?

(All in simplest form) ENGLISH | METRIC

1.   1 yd   2 ft   8 in   or   68 in
   + 2 yd   1 ft   6 in   or   90 in
      3 yd   3 ft   14 in =   158 in =
      4 yd   1 ft   2 in   4 yd 1 ft 2 in

2.   1 m   6 dm   7 cm   or   167 cm
   + 2 m   8 dm   5 cm   or   285 cm
      3 m   14 dm   12 cm =   452 cm =
      4 m   5 dm   2 cm   4 m 5 dm 2 cm

3.   5 ft   9 in
   +   3 ft   10 in
       yd   ft   in

4.   3 yd   2 ft
   + 1 yd   2 ft
      yd   ft

5.   3 m   9 dm
   + 2 m   6 dm
      m   dm

6.   4 m   27 cm
   +   4 m   78 cm
       m   dm   cm

7.   10 ft
   − 6 ft   3 in
      ft   in

8.   5 rd   1 ft
   − 1 rd   8 ft
      rd   ft

9.   3 km   2 hm
   − 1 km   7 hm
      km   hm

10.   8 cm   4 mm
   − 3 cm   6 mm
      cm   mm

11.   2 lb   3 oz
         ×6
     lb   oz

12.   lb   oz
   4 ⟌ 9 lb   4 oz

13.   6 g   4 dg
        ×3
     g   dg

14.   kg   hg
   4 ⟌ 9 kg   4 hg

15.   2 gal   2 qt   1 pt
             ×6
    gal   qt   pt

16.   gal   qt
   6 ⟌ 23 gal

17.   3 l 5 dl 5 cl 2 ml
                ×6
    l   dl   cl   ml

18.   l   dl
   5 ⟌ 23 l

19.   6 ft 6 in (rectangle, 3 ft 3 in height)

Find the area
_____ sq. ft.
_____ sq. in.
and check answer
(1 sq. ft. = 144 sq. in.)

20.   6 dm 6 cm (rectangle, 3 dm 3 cm height)

Find the area
_____ dm^2
_____ cm^2

21.   5 dollars   6 dimes   8 cents
      + 2 dollars   5 dimes   7 cents
         dollars   dimes   cents = $_____

TABLES OF CONVERSION

Metric SI ⟷ U.S. Customary
Systems International

Length

2.54 cm = 1 in
0.3048 m = 1 ft
.9144 m = 1 yd
1.609 km = 1 mi

* * * * *

1 mm = .03937 in
1 cm = .3937 in
1 m = 39.37 in
1 km = .621 mi

Weights or Masses

1 g = .035 oz (av)
1 dkg = .3527 oz
1 hg = 3.527 oz
1 kg = 2.205 lb

* * * * *

1 oz = 28.350 g
1 lb = 453.592 g
1 T = 0.907 metric ton
    1000 kg

Liquid Capacities or Volumes

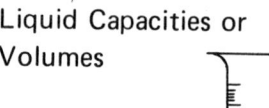

1 l = 1.057 liquid qt
    .908 dry qt
1 ml = 0.061 in^3
1 dal = 2.642 gal
    1.135 pk

* * * * *

1 pt = .550 l dry
    0.473 l liquid
1 qt = 1.101 l dry
    0.946 l liquid
1 gal = 3.785 l
1 pk = 8.810 l
1 bu = 35.239 l

Square Measure

1 cm^2 = .155 in^2
1 m^2 = 1.195 yd^2
1 m^2 = 10.763 ft^2

* * * * *

1 in^2 = 6.451 cm^2
1 ft^2 = .092 m^2
1 yd^2 = .836 m^2

Cubic Measure

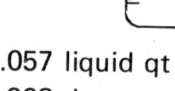

1 cm^3 = .061 in^3
1 m^3 = 1.307 yd^3
1 m^3 = 35.314 ft^3

* * * * *

1 in^3 = 16.387 cm^3
1 ft^3 = .028 m^3
1 yd^3 = .764 m^3

QUESTIONS ON CONVERSIONS Metric System ⇌ U. S. Customary

Use the converters and tables pages 71-82.

---

1. If you travel 30 km, is that farther than 30 miles?

2. The highway speed limit says:
   Will that speed in km per hour be a larger or a smaller number?

3. A liter carton of milk will fill four cups of milk?

4. If a 12 year old is 100 cm tall, could we call him shorty?

5. If you barbecued 1 kg of hamburger, would it fit nicely on the regular bun?

6. A 100 m run is (more or less) than a 100 yard run?

7. If your pop bottle contains 100 ml, Could you drink another 100 ml without feeling stuffed?

8. If your foot measures 100 mm, could we call you "Big Foot"?

9. A cubic yard of dirt is a little larger than a m³?

10. "A ton of bricks" in the metric system will be "a _____ kg of bricks."

11. "A mile long and a yard wide" should read, "a _____ km long and a _____ m wide."

    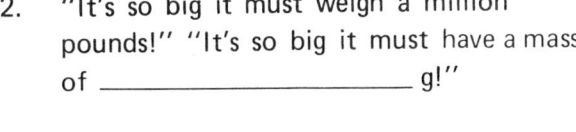

12. "It's so big it must weigh a million pounds!" "It's so big it must have a mass of _____ g!"

87

Metric System of Measurement © Activity Resources Co. Hayward, CA 94540

WHICH MEASUREMENT TO USE?

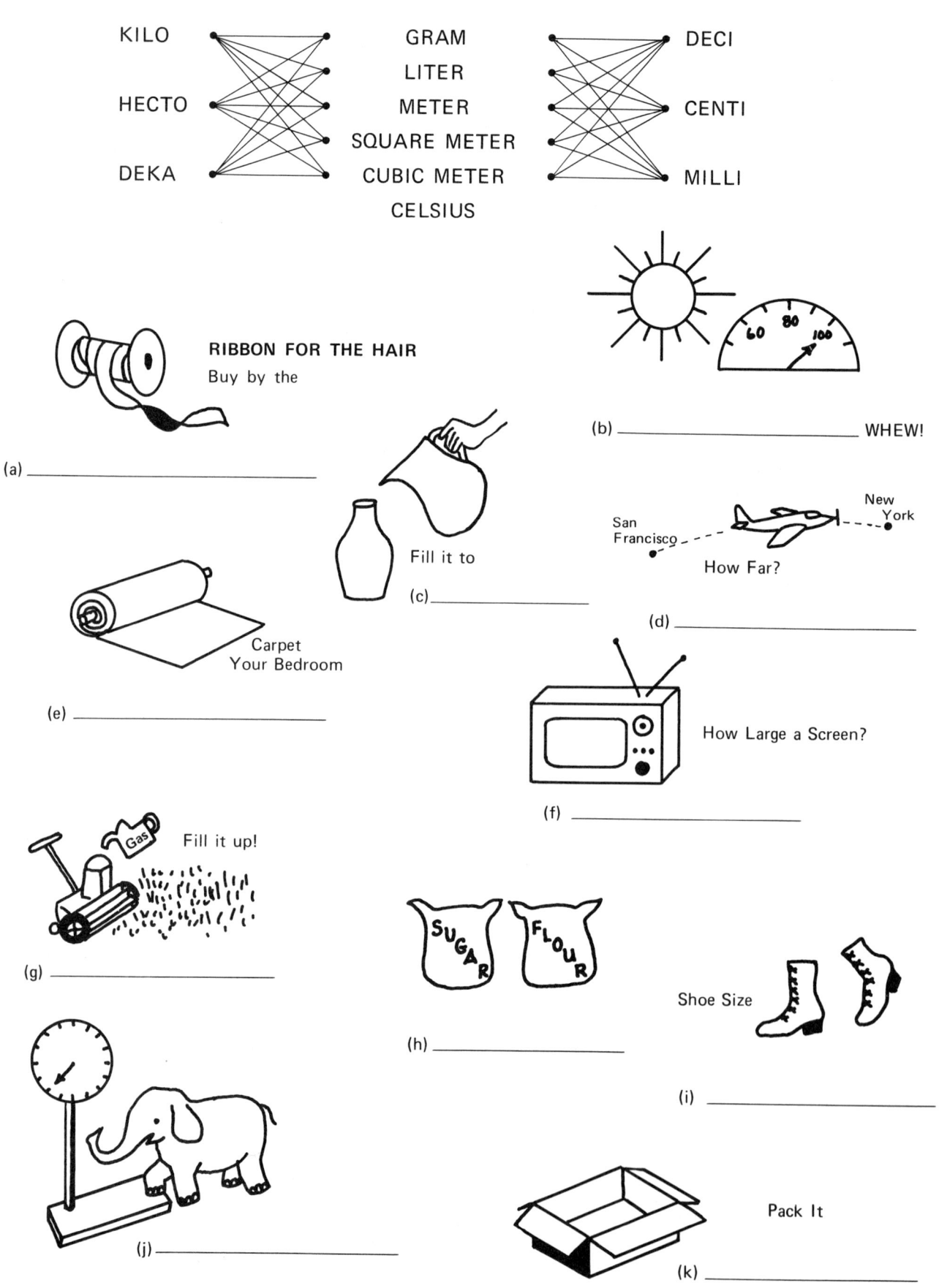

SECTION EIGHT

THE METROSCOPE

Use these two circular number lines for addition and subtraction problems using liters, meters, grams, money, base ten.

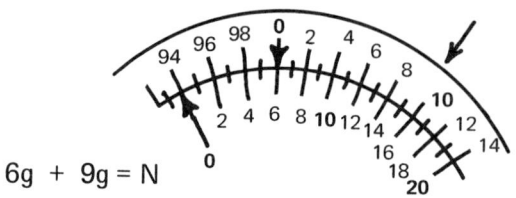

$6g + 9g = N$

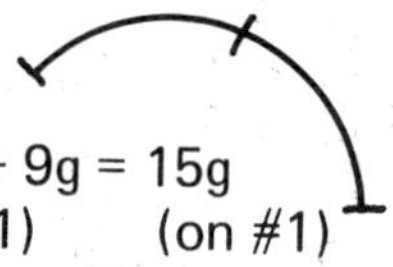

$6g + 9g = 15g$
(on #1)   (on #1)
  (on #2)

$15g - 6g = N$ $N = 1dg\ 5g\ or\ 15g$

$N = 9g$

$6g + Ng = 15g$ on #9
(on #1)
  (on #2)

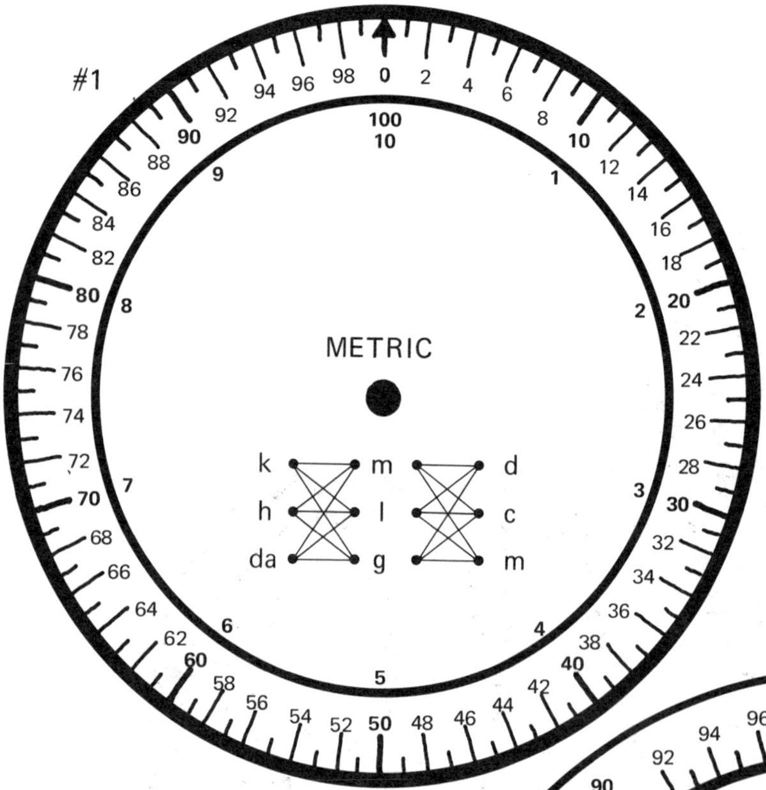

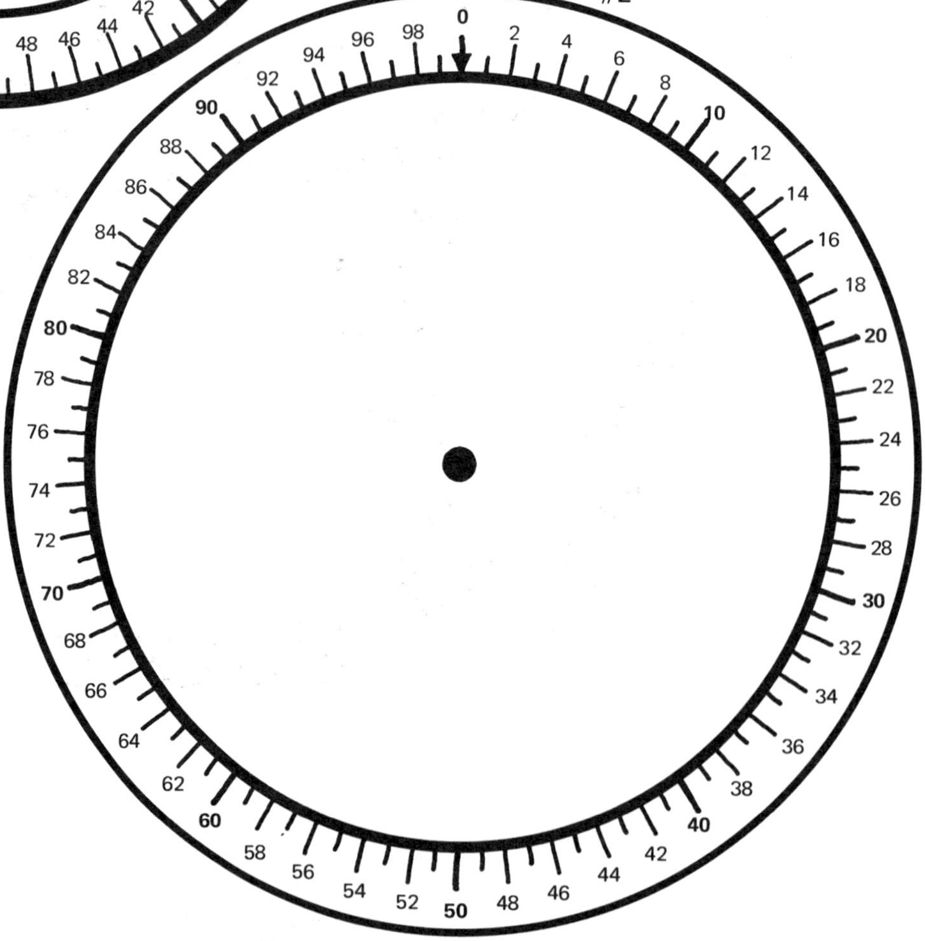

Cut out the 2 circles. Through the center use a snap, a grommet, or a brad to attach #1 on top of #2.

Metric System of Measurement © Activity Resources Co. Hayward, CA 94540

SOLVE WITH THE METROSCOPE

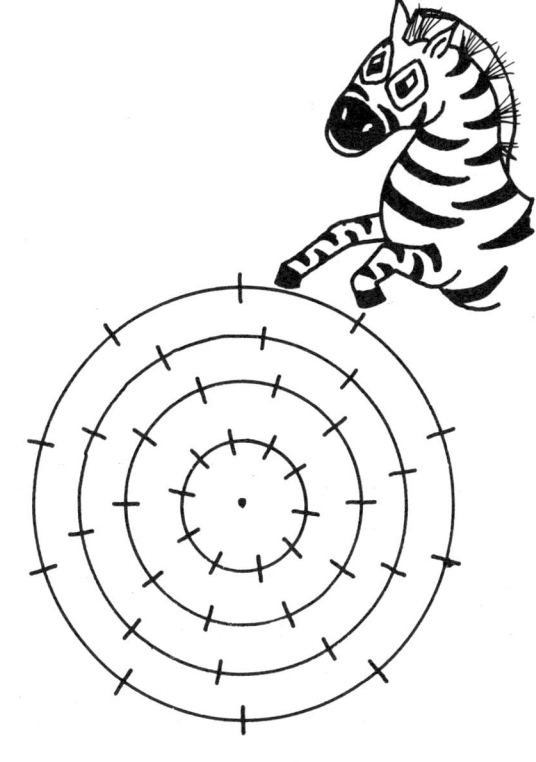

14mm + 38mm = _____ mm

82mm - 26mm = _____ cm

24l - 15l = _____ dl

37ml + 2.4dl = _____ dl

5.2km + 2.8km = _____ km

4.6g - 2.1g = _____ g

67pennies - 4 dimes = $ _____

88mg - 4.9cg = _____ g

7.4m + 2.9m = _____ dm

5.9cm + 17mm = _____ cm

* * * * * * * * * * * * *

14 + 29 + 27 = _____

6.3 + 2.3 + .6 = _____

.3 + .14 + .09 = _____

130 + 75 + 29 = _____

.023 + .018 + .05 = _____

Could these be
g ?
l ?
m ?
$?
. . . ?

FIND THE METRIC MEASUREMENT WORDS

Read: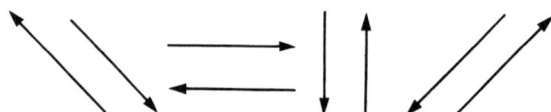

Can you find these words, prefixes that relate to measure in this puzzle?

C	I	B	U	C	M	W	X	A	L	H
A	N	I	U	Y	E	L	I	N	E	E
M	N	B	A	S	T	N	L	D	O	I
B	E	A	K	E	R	O	T	A	T	G
F	E	D	X	M	I	L	L	I	G	H
M	R	E	D	R	C	Z	E	B	N	T
E	U	C	A	S	S	S	A	M	O	U
T	T	I	H	O	Y	A	B	L	V	F
E	A	O	T	H	S	V	O	O	P	Y
R	R	C	A	F	T	E	L	A	C	S
T	E	P	R	I	E	U	I	Z	U	T
H	P	E	E	D	M	L	K	U	G	H
L	M	O	D	E	K	A	N	R	T	G
I	E	R	A	U	Q	S	I	G	R	I
T	T	A	R	X	E	D	N	S	Q	E
E	Y	Q	E	O	R	E	L	U	R	W
R	G	R	A	M	L	O	N	G	T	C

AREA
BEAKER
CENTI
CUBE
CUBIC
DECI
DEEP
DEKA
GRAM
GRID
HECTO
HEIGHT
KILO
LENGTH
LINE
LITER
LONG
MASS
METER
METRIC SYSTEM
MILLI
RULER
SCALE
SHORT
SQUARE
TEMPERATURE
UNIT
VOLUME
WEIGHT
WIDTH

WORD PUZZLES METRIC

The "Ten" game — Each word has a "TEN".

_ _ _ _ _	very uptight		_ _ _ _ _	he sings high
_ _ _ _ _ _ _	to put on mass pieces		_ _ _ _ _ _	make believe
_ _ _ _ _ _	A game with a raquet		_ _ _ _ _ _	a thin stem
i n T E N s i o n	goal, aim		_ _ _ _ _ _ _	one of the 50
_ _ _ _ _ _ _	feelers		_ _ _ _ _ _ _ _	scare

The "gram" game

_ _ _ _ _ _ _	a language book		_ _ _ _ _ _ _	a wire
_ _ _ _ _ _ _	entertainment		_ _ _ _ _ _ _	decorative initials
G R A M p u s	a killer whale		_ _ _ _ _	line drawing
_ _ _ _ _ _ _	a word game arranging letters		_ _ _ _ _ _	five pointed star

Exchange *one* letter for another and rescramble letters to form a metric system word or prefix.

	Remove Letter	Add Letter	Rescramble for Metric Word
MERIT	i	e	M _ _ _ _
DARE	r	_	_ _ _ _
LION	_	_	_ _ _ _
LIMIT	_	_	_ _ _ _ _
MARK	_	_	_ _ _ _
MILER	_	_	_ _ _ _ _
THOSE	_	_	_ _ _ _ _
CODE	_	_	_ _ _ _
SCENT	_	_	_ _ _ _ _

METRIC CROSS NUMBER PUZZLE

B   238 g + 108 g
F   731 km − 458 km
G   2 x 51 kl
H   8 dl = _____ cl
I   25 dimes = _____ pennies
K 8^3
Q   .42 kl = _____ l
S   5 x 70 mm
U   6 x 71 cg
W   2540 hm ÷ 4
Z   15 cm x 5 cm = _____ cm^2
BB 60 m x 6
CC (3 x 14 g) + (3 x 7 g)
dd 10^1
EE 30^2

a   .432 g = _____ mg
B   2790 km ÷ 9
C   4000 cg = _____ g
d 5^4
E   2 x 391 m
F   29 g = _____ mg
J   224 mm ÷ 4
L   126 cm ÷ 7
M 8^2
N   6 x 15 m = _____ m
O   91 mg ÷ 7

P   5 cm = _____ mm
R 3^3
T   696 kl ÷ 12
U   14 x 3 g
V   6 dg = _____ mg
W   3 x 213 dag = _____
X   .36 km = _____ m
Y   .5 g = _____ mg
Z   4566 g ÷ 6
aa 102 m − 49 m

AREA PUZZLE

14
13
5
5
8½
8
8

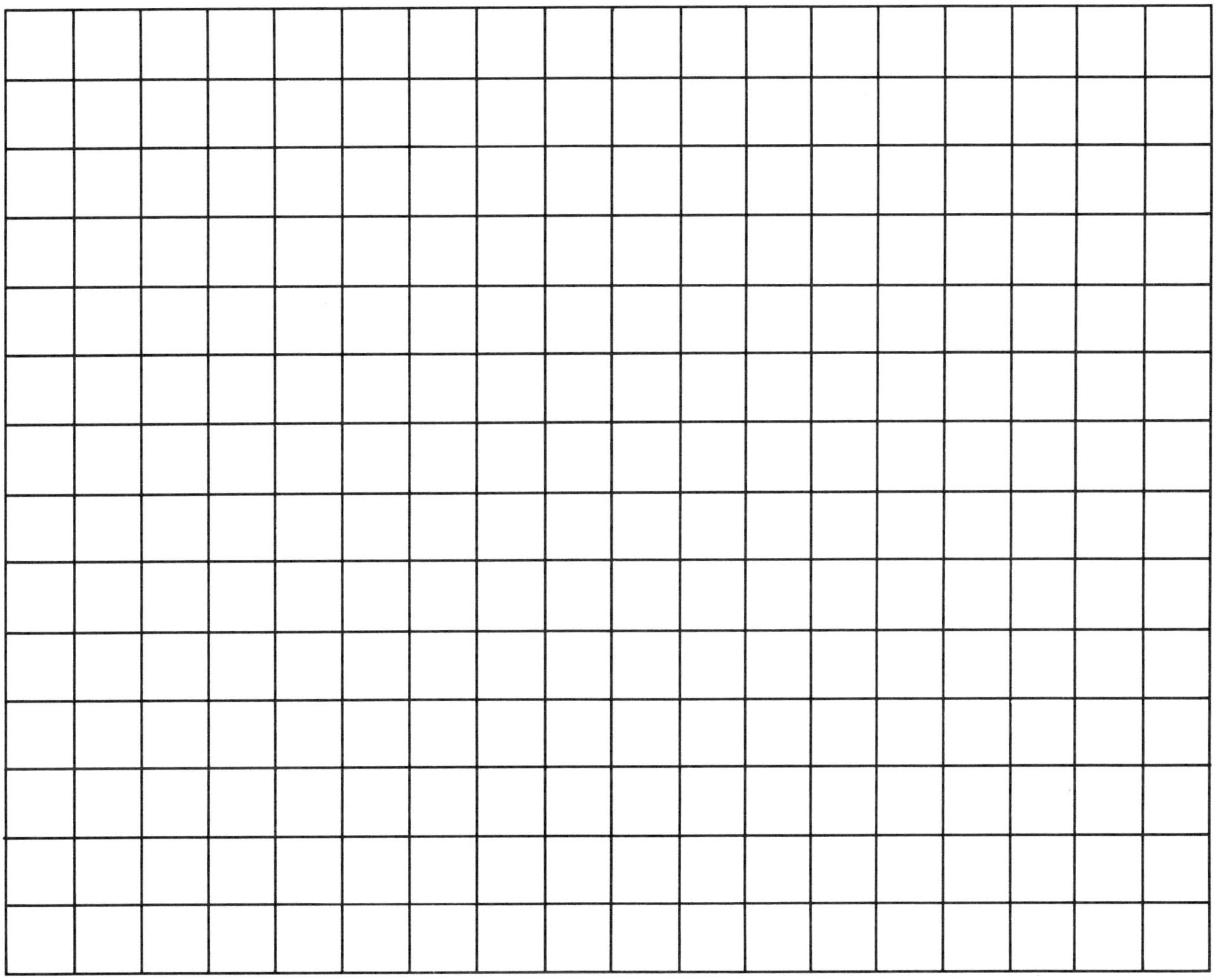

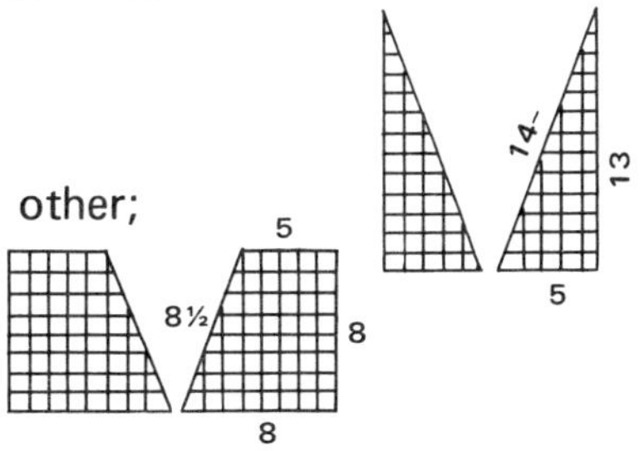

On the cm grid draw then cut out:

2 right triangles 5 cm by 13 cm that are mirror images of each other;

and

2 trapezoids 5 cm by 8 cm by 8 cm that are mirror images.

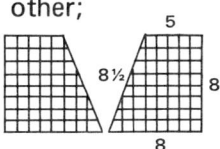

Arrange the 4 pieces in a square. The Area is ___________________

Arrange the 4 pieces in a rectangle. The Area is ___________________

Arrange the 4 pieces in an isosceles triangle. The Area is ___________________

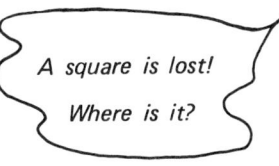

A square is lost!
Where is it?

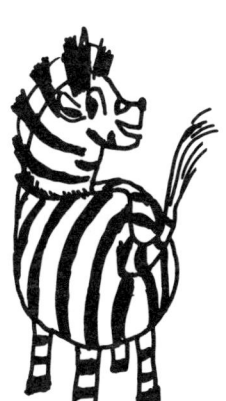

The Answers

SECTION NINE

ANSWER KEY *(Measurements for mm must be considered approximate.)*

Page

10. 4 cm, 5 cm, 2 cm, 5.5 cm, 4 cm, 15 cm, 11.5 cm, 10 cm

11. 25 mm, 100 mm, 70 mm, 8 mm, 42 mm, 52 mm, 67 mm, 100 mm, 150 mm, $\overline{BC}$, $\overline{HI}$, $\overline{IF}$

12.

mm	cm	dm
30	3	.3
50	5	.5
70	7	.7
100	10	1
15	1.5	.15
120	12	1.2
33	3.3	.33
47	4.7	.47

13.

(a)		(b)	
10	10	18	11
20	100	1.40	9.5
100	40	47	62
200	15		
18	80		

(c)	
50	7
11	930
7	63
15	3.8
370	4.5

14.

60	600	6,000
150	1500	15,000
380	3800	38,000
5	50	500
27	270	2,700
4.8	48	480
5.75	57.5	575
.6	6.0	60

16.

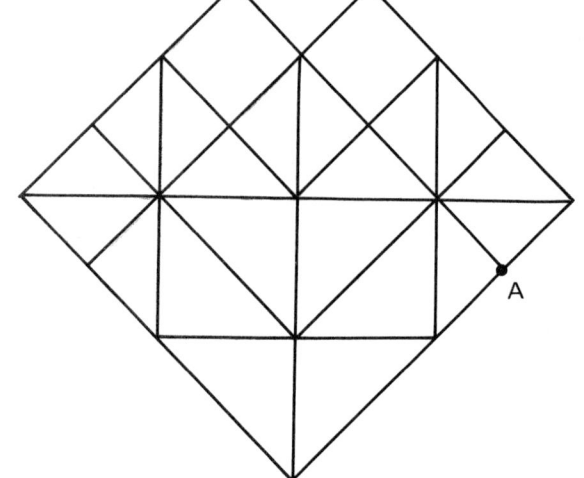

17.
a) 4 cm   4 cm
b) 50 mm   50 mm
c) 20 mm   20 mm
d) All are 2.6 cm
e) 21 mm   21 mm

18. 1.3 dm
1.2 dm
1.4 dm
19 cm
130 mm
80 mm
.3 dm

19.

▧ to ▶		10 cm
◯ to ⊓ to △		1.5 dm
# to $		7 cm
● to ●		13 cm
● to ▶		1.85 dm

20.

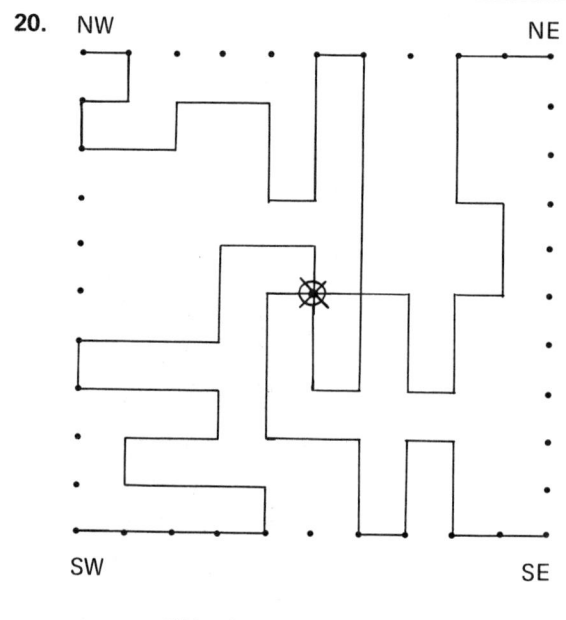

SW 24 cm = 240 mm
NE 20 cm = 200 mm
NW 22 cm = 220 mm
SE 16 cm = 160 mm

21.
a) 30 cm
b) 3.0 cm
c) 100 mm
d) 12 m
e) 1.25 m
f) 15 m
g) 98 cm

23.

93 km	75 km
98	71
96	71
130	113
28	28
106	61
551 km	419 km

24.

	mm	cm
a)	250	25.0
b)	200	20.0
c)	350	35.0
d)	135	13.5
e)	230	23.0

25.
11 cm
11 cm
15 cm
15 cm
7 cm
6 cm

26.

40 mm	30 mm
14 mm	15 cm
56 mm	1 - 9 - 3
156 mm	75 mm
102 mm	45 mm or 4.5 cm
159 mm	
71 mm	
45 mm	
24 mm	

98

Metric System of Measurement © Activity Resources Co. Hayward, CA 94540

ANSWERS

31.
a) ÷, ×
÷ 100, × 100
÷ 1000, × 1000
b) 1000 g
1000 l
c) .001
.001
d) g l
m m
l m^3
m^2 g

32.

	m	dm	cm	mm
a)	4.153	41.53	415.3	4153
b)	.630	6.30	63.0	630
c)	5.003	50.03	500.3	5003
d)	3.001	30.01	300.1	3001
e)	23.501	235.01	2350.1	23501
f)	42.160			
g)	2.034			
h)	250.201			

33.

a)	24.213	242.13	2421.3	24213
b)	3.052	30.52	305.2	3052
c)	0.304	3.04	30.4	304
d)	14.240	142.40	1424.0	14240
e)	50.023	500.23	5002.3	50023
f)	42.152	421.52	4215.2	42152
g)	1.025	10.25	102.5	1025
h)	0.325	3.25	32.5	325
i)	4.000	40.00	400.0	4000
j)	53.103	531.03	5310.3	53103

34.
a) 10, 100, 1000, 10, 100, 1000
b) 400, 250, 8000, 13500
c) .8, 2.7, 5.2, .9, .24, 4.3
d) 2,700, 500, 3,450,000
e) $1.47, $32.80, $1.68, $4.03, $.40, $.07
f) 248, 534, 28, 15,738, 5,209

35. a) $\frac{1}{100} = .01$, $\frac{50}{100} = \frac{1}{2} = .50 = .5$, $\frac{10}{100} = \frac{1}{10} = .10 = .1$, $\frac{20}{100} = \frac{1}{5} = .20 = .2$, $\frac{5}{100} = \frac{1}{20} = .05$, $\frac{14}{100} = \frac{7}{50} = .14$

		□	▦	▬	▤	⊥	⊞	Total	Prefix
b)	1 Meter	1 cm .1 dm .01 m	50 5 .5	10 1 .1	20 2 .2	5 .5 .05	14 1.4 .14	100 cm 10 dm 1 m	Centi Deci
c)	1 Gram	1 cm .1 dg .01 g	50 5 .5	10 1 .1	20 2 .2	5 .5 .05	14 1.4 .14	100 cg 10 dg 1 g	Centi Deci
d)	1 Liter	1 cl .1 dl .01 l	50 5 .5	10 1 .1	20 2 .2	5 .5 .05	14 1.4 .14	100 cl 10 dl 1 l	Centi Deci
e)	1 m^2	100 cm^2 1 dm^2 .01 m^2	5000 50 .5	1000 10 .1	2000 20 .2	500 5 .05	1400 14 .14	10,000 cm^2 100 dm^2 1 m^2	Centi Deci
f)	1 dm^2	100 mm^2 1 cm^2 .01 dm^2	5000 50 .5	1000 10 .1	2000 20 .2	500 5 .05	1400 14 .14	10,000 mm^2 100 cm^2 1 dm^2	Milli Centi Deci

ANSWERS

36.
1. a) 100 g = .1 kg
   b) 32 g = 32,000 mg
   c) 57 g = .057 kg
   ---
   d) 1 cg = .01 g
   e) .1 g = 1 dg = 100 mg
   f) .32 g = 320 mg

2. a) $.10 = 10¢
   b) 1 ¢ = $.01
   c) $.25 = 2.5 dimes
   ---
   d) 5¢ = .05$
   e) 10¢ = 1 dime
   f) 100¢ = 10 = 1$

37.
1. a) .30 = 3 ml
   b) .01 dl = .1 cl
   c) 1 cl = .01 l
   d) 17 ml = .017 l
   ---
   e) 17 l = 17,000 ml
   f) .010 kl = 10 l
   g) 42 l = 4200 cl
   h) .030 kl = 30,000 ml
   i) 100 l = .1 kl

2. a) 10 m = .01 km & 100 m = 1 hm
   b) 10 mm = 1 cm
   c) 100 mm = 1 dm
   ---
   d) .01 km = 10 m
   e) .1 km = 1 hm
   f) 0.89 km = 890 m

38.

7	7	.7
25	25	2.5
40	40	.4
890	890	8.9
6300	6300	6.3

39.

a)
1.9	1.9	.19	c) 38,600
60.3	60.3	6.03	2.570
56	56	.56	13.05
2430	2430	2.43	4,800
			2.9
			.0491

b)
110	110	11	650
120	120	12	.0013
190	190	19	.2
3,790	3,790	379	14.7
8,490	8,490	849	

4,700	4,700	47
5,900	5,900	59
97,000	97,000	97
256,000	256,000	256
50	50	.5

40.
$5 \times 5 = 25$
$8 \times 8 \times 8 = 512$
$6 \times 6 \times 6 \times 6 = 1296$
$1 \times 1 \times 1 \times 1 \times 1 \times 1 \times 1 = 1$
$9 \times 9 \times 9 = 729$
$3 = 3$

$(5 \times 10^6) + (2 \times 10^4) + (7 \times 10^1) + (5 \times 10^0)$
$(8 \times 10^2) + (7 \times 10^0)$
$(9 \times 10^5) + (2 \times 10^2)$
730,207
1,280
503,098

41.

10^2	10^6	10^7
10^6	10^3	10^0
10^6	10^2	10^1
10^1	10^5	10^3
10^0	10^4	10^2
10^1	10^0	10^1

$(5 \times 10^{-1}) + (1 \times 10^{-2}) + (3 \times 10^{-3})$
5006.04
430.109

10^{-4}	10^{-1}	10^2
10^{-2}	10^{-3}	10^{-4}
10^1	10^1	10^{-2}

42.
8 cm^2
9 cm^2
10 cm^2
72 cm^2
36 cm^2
56 cm^2
63 cm^2
64 cm^2
96 cm^2
135 cm^2
9 cm^2
17.5 cm^2
15 cm^2 3 cm
360 cm^2 2 cm
480 cm^2 3 cm

44. $100 \text{ cm}^2 = 1 \text{ dm}^2$

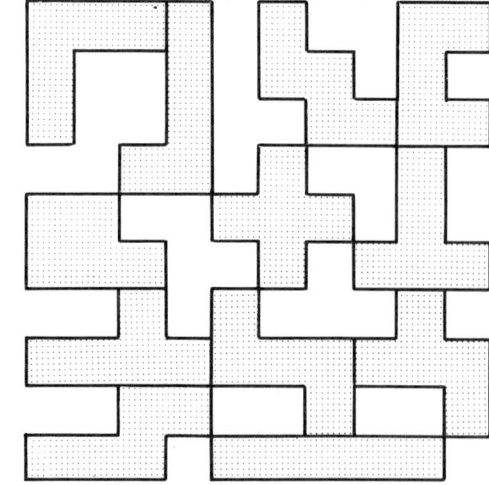

12 Different Shapes

ANSWERS

45. $4 \times 4 = 4^2 = 16$
$5 \times 5 = 5^2 = 25$
$6 \times 6 = 6^2 = 36$
1, 4, 9, 16, 25, 36, 49, 64, 81, 100,
1, 3, 5, 7, 9, 11, 13, 15, 17, 19
Odd

46.
300	6
900	18
1500	47
2100	29
1.5	360
2.4	720
3.7	1435
15.32	9007

47.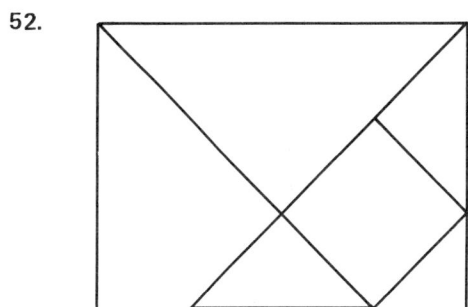
$A = 7.5$ cm^2
$P = 13.8$ cm

$A = 12$ cm^2
$P = 16$ cm

$A = 14$ cm^2
$P = 30$ cm

50.
$P = 40$ cm
$A -$
a $= 9$ cm^2
b $= 12$ cm^2
c $= 12$ cm^2
d $= 12$ cm^2
$\cap = 5$ cm^2
$\cup = 40$ cm^2
Ext. $= 60$ cm^2

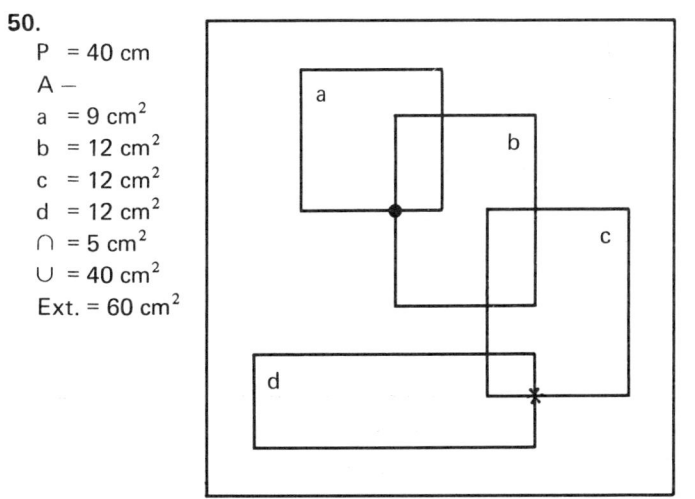

51. $P = 70$ cm $A = 66$ cm^2
$A = 34$ cm^2

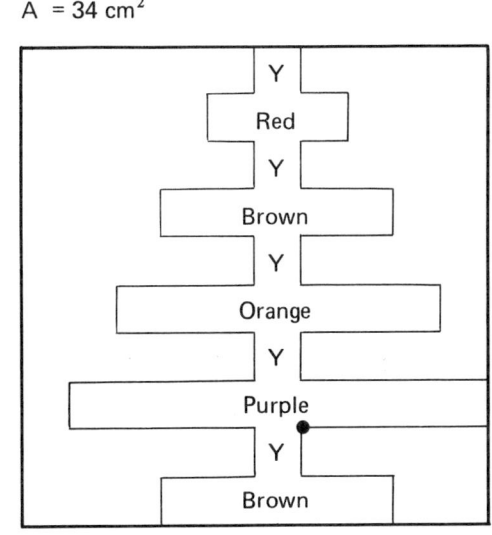

52.

1) 14 cm   10) 5 cm
2) 5 cm   11) 24.5 About
3) 5 cm   6.125
4) 7 cm   24.5
6) 10.5 cm   6.125
7) 7 cm   12.5
   3.5 cm   12.5
8) 3.5 cm   12.25
                     98.5

53.
a)	32 m^2	24 m
b)	9 cm	36 cm
c)	11 km	110 km^2
d)	8 m	⟷ 9 m
e)	14 km	⟷ 3 km
f)	9 cm	68 km
g)	11 mm	⟷ 13 mm
h)	18 dm	198 dm^2
i)	1200 mm^2	160 mm
	12 cm^2	16 cm
j)	4 m	⟷ 17 m

54. Answers may vary slightly

ANSWERS

55. Answers may vary slightly
- Living Room — 24 m²
- Bedroom A — 12 m²
- B — 12 m²
- C — 12 m²
- Master — 14.5 m²
- Bath A — 4.5 m²
- B — 3.5 m²
- Linen & Closets — 2 m²
- Kitchen & Family — 35.5 m²
- Hall & Closet — 10 m²
- Gargae — 45 m²
- Total — 175 m²

57.
9 cm²	5 cm
12 cm²	7 cm
49 cm²	8 cm
54 cm²	5 cm
5 cm²	10 cm
24 cm²	9 cm
36 cm²	5 cm
60 cm²	8 cm
64 cm²	8 cm
21 cm²	10 cm
	Yes

60.
8
24
18
1,000
2,000
12,000
3
5
43,000
14
.5
3,500

61.
a) 2, 2 cm³
b) 3 × 3 × 3 = 27, 27 cm³
c) 2 × 2 × 3 = 12, 12 cm³
d) 4 × 3 × 3 = 36, 36 cm³
e) 2 × 4 × 5 = 40, 40 cm³
f) 144 cm³
480 cm³
525 m³
484 km³
1 dm³
168 dm³

62.
24	2	2 × 2 × 6	
		2 × 4 × 3	
60	4	2 × 3 × 10	2 × 2 × 15
		2 × 6 × 5	4 × 3 × 5
72	6	2 × 2 × 18	4 × 6 × 3
		2 × 4 × 9	8 × 3 × 3
		2 × 3 × 12	2 × 6 × 6
100	3	2 × 2 × 25	4 × 5 × 5
		2 × 5 × 10	
84	4	2 × 6 × 7	4 × 3 × 7
		2 × 2 × 21	2 × 3 × 14

63.
1	1	1	1
8	4	2	1
27	9	3	1
64	16	4	1
125	25	5	1
216	36	6	1
343	49	7	1
512	64	8	1
729	81	9	1
1000	100	10	1
1331	121	11	1
1728	144	12	1
b^3	b^2	b^1	1 or b^0

67.
a) 1000
3000
.5
.238
1,754
4
29
2
2000
1.5
1.5

b)
105 cm³   .105 l
36 cm³   .036 l
480 dm³   480 l
720 dm³   720 l
192,000 dm³   192,000 l
180 m³   180 kl

c) 1 × 1 × 4 dm
1 × 2 × 2 dm
1 × 1 × 83 dm
2 × 2 × 3 dm
1 × 4 × 3 dm
1 × 2 × 6 dm
1 × 1 × 12 dm

69.
No
About ¼
2 in a glass
24
1.9 ml
250 ml
125 km

70.
30 l of water
45 l of gas
6.705 l or 6705 ml
90 kl or 90,000 l

ANSWERS

72.	.380	1000	**73.**	a. 18 cm^3	.018 l	18 g	.018 kg	**75.**	a. and b. answers will vary
	2.5	870		b. 168 cm^3	.168 l	168 g	.168 kg		c. No
	5700	.0246		c. 324 cm^3	.324 l	324 g	.324 kg		d. The shape of an object doesn't influence the weight.
	912	.22		Tower 510 cm^3	.510 l	510 g	.510 kg		
	4000	170							
	1800	1570							
	3.5	24.6							
	7.652	5.3							

78.
- 194°F
- 75°C
- 60°C
- 122°F
- 40°C
- 77°F
- 50°F

79.
1. No
2. No
3. No
4. Right
5. Wrong
6. Yes
7. Right
8. No
9. Wrong
10. Wrong

80.
- 2.5
- 2
- 8.8
- 5.2
- 5.9
- 21.3
- 50.8
- 16.8

81.
A	190	100
B	110	30
C	160	55
D	125	43
E	175	78
F	140	50

82.
- >100
- >900
- <1100
- <600
- >1
- <.7
- <1.3
- = .456

83.
- >1
- >1
- <88
- >3
- <3.5
- <40
- >16
- = 1.057

2 qt, 9 c, 5 pt, 11 c, 3 qt, 13 c, 7 pt, 15 c, 17 c, 9 pt

84.
1. 1.6 km
2. .4 km
3. 2 mi, 3.2 km
4. 38.4 km
5. 71'' – 5'11''
6. 6.4 m (about)
7. 2.3 kg (about)
8. 5.18 m
9. 40°C

87.
1. No
2. Larger
3. Right
4. Yes
5. No
6. More
7. Yes
8. No
9. No
10. 1000
11. 1.609 km .9144 m
12. 453,529,000 g

85.
3. 3 yd 0 ft 7 in
5. 6m 5 dm
7. 3 ft 9 in
9. 1 km 5 hm
11. 13 lb 2 oz
13. 19 g 2 dg
15. 15 gal 3 qt 0 pt
17. 21 l 3 dl 1 cl 2 ml
19. 21.125 sq ft
   3042 sq. in
21. 7, 11, 15 = $8.25

4. 5 yd 1 ft
6. 9 m 0 dm 5 cm
8. 3rd 9½ ft
10. 4 cm 8 mm
12. 2 lb 5 oz
14. 2 kg 3.5 hg
16. 3 gal 3⅓ qt
18. 4 l 6 dl
20. 21.78 dm^2
    2178 cm^2

88.
a. m or cm
b. Celsius
c. ml
d. km
e. m^2
f. cm^2
g. l
h. kg or g
i. cm
j. kg
k. m^3

91.
52 mm	103 dm
5.6 cm	7.6 cm
90 dl	70
2.77 dl	9.2
8 km	.53
2.5 g	234
$.27	.091
.039 g	

ANSWERS

92.

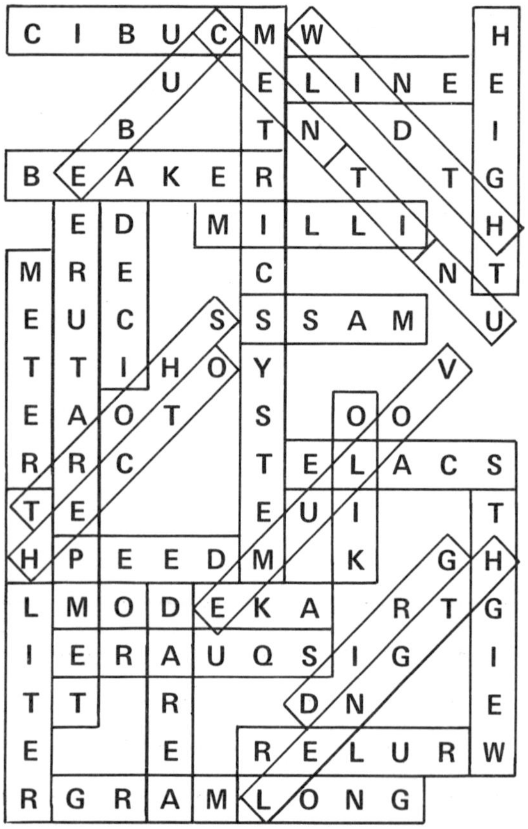

93.

Tense	Tenor
Fatten	Pretend
Tennis	Tendril
Intension	Tennessee
Antennae	Frighten
or	
Tentacle	

Grammar	Telegram
Program	Monogram
Grampus	Diagram
Anagrams	Pentagram

Meter
Deka
Kilo
Milli
Gram
Liter
Hecto
Deci
Centi

94.

	4		3	4	6		7	
2	7	3		1	0	2	8	0
5		2	5	0		5	1	2
0			6			8		
0		6		9		1		5
0		4	2	0		3	5	0
			7			8		
4	2	6		6	3	5		7	5
2		0		3	6	0		6	3
		1	0		9	0	0		1

95. A ☐ = 169 cm²

A ▭ = 168 cm²

A △ = 168 cm²